Boxcar Diplomacy

Two Trains that Crossed the Ocean

Jane Sweetland

ISBN 978-1-54396-044-0

Dedicated to Gabrielle Griswold
whose memories brought this story to life.

Acknowledgements

I began this book because I was curious, but I finished it because I was inspired. Inspiration came from the story itself, but also from the many people I met as I began to research. I owe each and every one a debt of gratitude. One of my first contacts was Dorothy Scheele, curator of the Friendship Train 1947 website, who graciously shared with me hundreds of index cards on which she had recorded her research. I met Gabrielle Griswold, who had lived in France after the war, where she worked with American Aid to France and was the secretary for the Friendship Train in France. What a delight to hear her memories! After meeting, Gabrielle and I began corresponding and she shared with me her album of newspaper clippings and photos and, of course, many stories of France in those years.

I have also relied on the research and scholarship of Alexis Muller, curator of the Merci Train Facebook site, and an insightful bilingual and bicultural guide in my quest. Alexis shared with me many of the white papers he has compiled as well as raw research that has yet to be understood. I also want to thank Christian Vilnas, whose well-curated website is rich with links, all of which I gratefully accessed.

In France, I had delightful meetings and much correspondence with Guy Jouteaux, curator of Le Musée Bouchardais, not far from Paris. Guy has collected and exhibited many train artifacts and he provided me with many documents and insightful conversations. In Paris I was so happy to meet Christian Huart, the son of Georges Huart who had sailed in the Magellan across the Atlantic. Christian was just ten when the ship sailed, but he remembered well his father leaving and returning and he still has a set of the Robert Louis shields created for the Merci boxcars. I so enjoyed hearing his memories of France at that time.

At the Capitol Museum in Phoenix, I had the great good fortune of being able to work with registrar, Stephanie Mahon, and researcher, Carissa Whiting, whose knowledge of the gifts made for a productive, interesting, and fun visit. That experience was mirrored many times over in the Nevada State Museum in Carson City, where Sue Ann Monteleone, and Mary Covington allowed me access to the archives and the many notes that accompanied the gifts. In the last many months, Mary has been an invaluable colleague, answering countless questions and always ready to help in the quest for true stories of both trains.

From the Friendship Train, it was not a long bridge to the Merci Train website, where I promptly purchased Earl Bennett's account of his travels as he searched to find every boxcar. Though Earl passed away in 2013, researchers continue to owe Earl our gratitude. Thanks to Roxanne Godsey, Earl's website continues today. I also relied on Roxanne's research in the Drew Pearson archives in the LBJ Library in Austin, Texas for many of the primary documents I cited here. John and Sue Ann Irving and their group of intrepid explorers who have visited most of the boxcars have been generous in sharing their knowledge, photos and encouragement for this project. Danielle Saunders provided invaluable translations and research for my visit to France and registrars and researchers at state museums nationwide have been patient, gracious, and ever willing to answer yet one more question.

Finally, to my friends and family, my early readers and editors: Thank you. Without you, the book would have been pot-holed with mysterious sentences that needed context. A bouquet of thanks is due especially to my husband, Lee Edwards, and my daughter, Haley Sweetland Edwards, who read the manuscript several times as it was a work-in-progress and each time made it better. Your encouragement means the world to me.

The building that was once the L'Ile-Bouchard train station is today the Musée du Bouchardais, where I enjoyed meeting the proprietor, Guy Jouteux, who provided me with many insights into the French side of this story.

Contents

BOOK ONE – THE FRIENDSHIP TRAIN

Part I.

1. A Man with an Idea

On October 11, 1947, a patriotic, peace-loving, controversial Quaker newspaperman named Drew Pearson published a column that inspired Americans. His idea was that people should begin scraping together to send food to war-ravaged Europeans, millions of whom were starving in the aftermath of World War II. What made Pearson's idea so compelling was that it was both modest and audacious. He was not beseeching the United States government to create a new foreign aid project, nor was he demanding that the international community join in a massive new humanitarian effort. He was, instead, simply calling upon individual Americans—mothers and fathers, children and neighbors, insurance salesmen, bowling leagues and Little League teams—to save food from their kitchen tables, pantries, gardens and farms and give it to their brethren across the Atlantic, who were desperately in need. The effort, he wrote, would represent "a genuine sacrifice from the heart of America."

In the October column, Pearson suggested that if there were enough interest in this idea, perhaps a freight train could be arranged. It would begin in California, he mused, and snake its way across the country, collecting donations of flour, beans, evaporated milk, macaroni, sugar and wheat from communities along the way. The train would end at the New York Harbor, where its contents would be loaded on a ship destined for war-ravaged France. Pearson called his seed of an idea the "Friendship Train."

But on the day his column hit newsstands nationwide, it was little more than a thought experiment. There were no communities clamoring to donate, no boxes of macaroni, no freight train to speak of. If the idea in his column turned out to strike a nerve, Pearson had no idea how he'd pull it off.

2. A Friendship Train

Pearson's column didn't materialize out of thin air. The week before it was published, President Truman had launched a new government entity, the "Citizens Food Committee," which he tasked with the job of getting Americans to eliminate food waste. If Americans could conserve the food they were currently throwing out, Truman argued, there would be surplus to send to Europe.

Pearson's subsequent *Washington Merry-go-Round* column was written as an open letter to Charles Luckman, the chairman of the new Citizens Food Committee. In the column, Pearson wasn't exactly critical of the effort. He really liked the idea in principle. The problem, he wrote, was that it stopped short: it wasn't enough to just encourage Americans to waste less food. They needed to understand *why* they should conserve flour and sugar and beans and *why* sending food across the ocean mattered in the first place. And in order to do that, they needed to understand the geopolitical stakes.

In that column, Pearson described a dangerously divided world in the post-WWII years, riven by the creep of communism. Already, Europe was being divided between the eastern communist states and the western democracies. Americans, Pearson wrote, must understand their efforts to send food to Europeans in that political context. Their actions are not only humanitarian, they are politically strategic.

Pearson described the status quo as a cautionary tale. After all, the U.S. government and dozens of American charities were already sending vast quantities of food to Europe. But they were doing so quietly, so efficiently that many Europeans didn't know that the U.S. was donating any food at all. Meanwhile, the Union of Soviet Socialist Republics (U.S.S.R.), which was sending a fraction of what the U.S. was, had made a point of showing off its largesse with pomp and fanfare. "In Marseille harbor, a cargo of Soviet wheat entered with flags flying," Pearson wrote. "There were street parades, a municipal holiday and paeans of praise for the great benefactors of the

French people – Soviet Russia." Simultaneously, in Le Havre, several thousand tons of America's wheat, many times that given by Russia, "was unloaded efficiently and unostentatiously."[1]

The U.S., in other words, was losing the propaganda war against the U.S.S.R., Pearson warned, and suggested that the Friendship Train could help bridge the gap. Instead of just asking people, as Truman's Citizens Food Committee proposed to do, to waste less and quietly give more food to Europe, Pearson's train would be a public relations spectacular. People could watch the progress of the "Friendship Train" in the newspaper and hear it on the radio as it traveled from the West Coast, across the Rockies and through the heartland, collecting boxcars filled with food for Europe at every station along the way. They could imagine their gifts rumbling all the way to the docks in New York Harbor where they would be loaded on a ship and sent across the Atlantic. Pearson figured that if individuals one by one, club by club and town by town contributed a little, it would add up to a lot. At every station there could be parades and a grand send-off and people could see that their bag of flour was part of something much bigger. The Friendship Train would generate well-deserved publicity; it would be an event to rival the Soviets' display of altruism in Marseille.

---

[1] *Drew Pearson, Washington Merry-go-Round nationally syndicated column, October 11, 1947. He also hosted a weekly radio show on Sundays.*

On October 11, 1947, Drew Pearson published a nationally syndicated column suggesting that Americans should help Europeans who had experienced the ravages of war, a freezing winter, and summer drought. (The editor's note is dated the day before publication in most newspapers nationwide.) Clipping of The Daily Argus-Leader, Sioux Falls, South Dakota, from newspapers.com.

3. Waste Makes Want / Want Makes War!

In June 1947, four months before Pearson's column was published, Secretary of State George C. Marshall gave a commencement speech at Harvard calling on the government to create an economic recovery program for Europe. This idea, which became known as the "Marshall Plan," would help European nations rebuild their own economies with an infusion of U.S. capital. It was a powerful proposal, but it came at a tough time for both American and international politics.

17

The U.S.S.R., deeply skeptical of U.S. foreign policy efforts, condemned the Marshall Plan as a capitalist plot. Joseph Stalin, dictator of the U.S.S.R., later refused to allow the eastern bloc countries to participate. Americans weren't all that enthusiastic either. In 1947, America's own economy was struggling. The collapse of military spending had sent the U.S. Gross National Product (GNP) spiraling downward, inflation ticking upward, and labor strikes rolled across the nation. Over Truman's veto, the Republican Congress passed legislation curbing workers' right to strike and American families faced shortages of meat, chicken and eggs.

But Europeans were in even worse shape. Millions had been left homeless by the war, state treasuries were exhausted, crop yields were lower than they had been since Napoleon's reign 130 years before, and milk was so severely rationed it was available only to young children so that they could grow healthy teeth. The U.S. had enough surplus to send 470 million bushels of grain, but severe cold, floods, and drought had so reduced grain production in Europe that 100 million additional bushels were needed to keep people from starving. Where could Americans find that kind of surplus?

That's where Truman's Citizens Food Committee idea had come from. Armed with statistics showing that ten percent of what Americans fed to their livestock or brought home to eat was wasted, Truman urged Americans to help make up the 100-million-bushel deficit by conserving, being more efficient, wasting less. The ad slogan for the new Citizens Food Committee was ominous: "Waste Makes Wants / Want Makes

War!" As Secretary of State Marshall explained at the time, "Hunger and insecurity are the worst enemies of peace. For recovery and political stability, Europe needs many things, but the most elemental, indispensable need is food." Truman appointed Charles Luckman, a businessman and advertising whiz, to head up the new Citizens Food Committee and the day it was announced, *The New York Times* featured a photo of the two men on the front page, above the fold.

Pearson was on his farm on the Potomac when he caught news of the new effort. He liked the idea—he could see plenty of food waste in his own small agricultural operation, but he was immediately seized with the idea of getting Americans *personally* engaged in the effort. If they saw at least some of their sacrifice in action and felt like they were part of a team—Team America—they could really make a difference.

He also liked the idea of a program that wasn't spearheaded, authorized, or funded by the government. Part of the appeal of a community-driven campaign was to show the communists who were agitating in Western Europe what a free people living in a democracy could do without government permission or support. Food is a form of soft power and Pearson thought that a bottom-up, grassroots effort would feel more real and be more powerful than a top-down, government led endeavor. The Friendship Train, in his imagination of it could simply be a vessel bearing gifts from one people to another. He liked the geniality of the whole idea. "There is another thing about this new instrument of foreign policy that is important," Pearson would later write. "It fits into the

American scheme of things. It's just as friendly as individual Americans."[2]

Even though the Friendship Train was not associated with the government, Pearson hoped to leverage the vast reach of the Citizens Food Committee's new advertising campaign. That's why he decided to publish the idea of a Friendship Train as an open letter to Mr. Luckman: he could support the government's campaign to conserve, while offering a private solution that allowed people to imagine the power of their personal sacrifice.

4. Powered by Influence

Pearson was well connected through his daily nationally syndicated daily column and weekly radio broadcast, so he knew he would have no problem promoting the idea. But first, before gauging public reaction, he needed a "National Friendship Train Committee" and he needed it to be packed with opinion leaders. He didn't want financial support from the government, but he needed to know that the government would not create administrative hurdles. He knew that if he could get leaders, there would be followers.

On the very day the Food Committee was headline news, Pearson started making phone calls from the farm to build a committee. Harry M. Warner, one of the four co-founding brothers of the motion picture company, Warner Brothers Studios, agreed to act as chair. No financial support from the

---

[2] *Merry-G-Round, November 8, 1947.*

government was asked for or given, but elected and appointed officials including representatives and senators from both parties, and the Secretaries of Agriculture and Labor agreed to do what they could to support the effort. To cap off a celebrity roster of the politically connected, Pearson created two honorary chairs: one for Eleanor Roosevelt, the other for Senator Alben W. Barkley, the Democratic leader in Congress.[3]

Civic organizations (Jaycees, Lions, Kiwanis, and Rotary) were each represented by their presidents. Labor, too, had a prominent place at the table as leaders of the AFL, CIO, and the Brotherhoods of Railway and Steamship Clerks and Railroad Trainmen agreed to serve. Exactly who among his many contacts had confirmed their commitment to the Friendship Train between October 1 when the Citizens Food Committee was launched and October 11 when his column was published is not clear, but he had certainly laid the groundwork for a powerful new project. The tricky bit was he hadn't heard from the railroads. Without trains, collecting food from small towns across America and getting it to Europe would be impossible.

---

[3] *National Friendship Committee members included Representatives Sol Bloom, D-NY and Charles Eaton R-NJ, Senators Tom Connally (D-TX) Charles F. Brannan, the Assistant Secretary of Agriculture; Maurice J. Tobin, Secretary of Labor; and Charles Luckman, President of the Citizens Food Committee. Eleanor Roosevelt, and Senator Alben W. Barkley, were honorary members. Presidents of Civic Organizations: Paul D. Bagwell (Jaycees); Eugene S. Briggs (Lions Club); J. Belmont Mosser (Kiwanis) and Harry Schmedes (Rotary). Labor leaders: William Green (AFL), George M. Harriman (Brotherhood of Railway and Steamship Clerks), Philip Murray (CIO), and A.F. Whitney (Brotherhood of Railroad Trainmen).*

5. Waiting for the Railroads

Pearson approached the American Railroad Association in the days before he published his column, but his request could not be easily answered. One problem was that in the United States, train management is complicated. The American Railroad Association is a network of dozens of freight carriers, which collectively cover the entire nation, but there is no single national railroad. So, when Pearson requested a train that would cross eleven states and wend its way from California to New York, he needed not only available freight cars, but also the cooperation and participation of railroad executives and workers from at least five railroads: Southern Pacific, Union Pacific, Northwestern, Pennsylvania and New York Central.

To further complicate matters, Pearson didn't know exactly what he was asking for. He had no idea how many freight cars his campaign would actually need. He hoped that as the train trundled across the country, Americans would fill a total of 180 cars because that would mean that the train was a mile long. It's a poetic number, and a grand image—180 freight cars loaded by people from nearly every state rolling from the Pacific Ocean across the Continental Divide and the Great Plains to the Atlantic shore. But a mile-long train meant collecting at least a thousand tons from every state through which the train would cross.[4] Would states not on the route

---

[4] *The calculation of tonnage is based on 62.5 tons per freight car, which is the tonnage quoted by the Santa Fe Railroad for capacity of their freight cars at the time. Pearson himself suggested that his goal was a mile-long train, which he calculated to be 180 cars in length. That may have been true; however, Wendell Huffman, historian at the Nevada Railroad Museum said that the average boxcar at that time was 45 feet, so 120 cars would have measured a mile.*

send donations to a station in another state where their contribution could be coupled to the train? Pearson didn't know the answers to any of these questions.

He also wasn't at all sure he could pull it off by his self-imposed deadline: The Friendship Train, he had decided, should arrive in France by Christmas. He had chosen that date because it added meaning for many in the U.S. and Europe and also, perhaps, because Christmas is not a holiday sanctioned by communist regimes. It was already October and it would take a month of travel just to get the train from the Pacific to the Atlantic, loaded aboard a ship, and delivered across the ocean to France. Once the ship docked in Le Havre, more time would be necessary because in Pearson's vision, at least some of America's Christmas gift should be ceremoniously received at the dock and a token distribution should be made throughout France. He wanted crowds and speeches, and cameras rolling. And the whole party needed to happen by Christmas.

6. Muckraker and Patriot

Pearson wrote a daily column, which was nationally syndicated and widely read, but he was not well-respected by fellow journalists, who suggested that he got the facts right about sixty percent of the time. Pearson was a pro-Franklin Delano Roosevelt Democrat and had favored much of the President's agenda, but he wasn't always on the President's good side. After labeling Roosevelt "anti-Russian," FDR called Pearson a "chronic liar." It was a criticism that might have brought many in the media to Pearson's defense, but *Time* magazine reported that the press was slow to react to Roosevelt's accusations. "Drew Pearson, the capital's No. 1 gossip columnist, is not popular with his colleagues. He has always had good sources in the State and Justice Departments and has produced many an authentic news beat...But he is frequently guilty of colossal errors of fact, often reports cocktail gossip as gospel truth, sometimes writes colossal fictions."[5] One reviewer of an unauthorized biography wrote, "Basically his column was entertainment designed to hold the biggest possible crowd in the main tent. Pearson was more showman than newsman."[6]

Pearson himself would agree that he was a showman. He had learned the art of public speaking when he was a teenager, helping his father on the Chatauqua Circuit, a late nineteenth, early twentieth century forum that looked a lot like a circus, except instead of clowns and elephants, there were performers and politicians, writers and activists who traveled through rural America. As a boy, then as a young man, Drew helped his father set up the tents, promote the event, and entertain the crowds. The Friendship Train was in many ways a perfect example of Pearson's impresario skillset. In fact, in late 1948, Pearson submitted an application to a competition sponsored by *Variety,* seeking recognition for the series of broadcasts

---

[5] *Time Magazine, U.S. At War: Chronic Liar, Sept. 13, 1943*
[6] *New York Times archive, William V. Shannon, "The Sol Hurok of the Washington press corps," April 29, 1973.*
https://www.nytimes.com/1973/04/29/archives/drew-pearson-an-unauthorized-biography-by-oliver-pilat-illustrated.html, accessed July 10, 2018. Sol Hurok was a Russian immigrant who became an impresario in New York, well-known for his shows as well as his showmanship.

about the Friendship Train as a "noteworthy example of radio showmanship."[7]

But if calling someone a showman sounds like criticism in the modern context, Pearson was not a political carnival-barker. He may have cultivated the limelight, but it was often in the service of a deeply held moral conviction. As Felicia Cameron, Pearson's granddaughter, said her grandfather "was more than a showman. He was also a civil and social activist who went after a lot of crooked people. For them, he took the gloves off."[8]

7. Behind the Scenes

The weeks after Pearson published his October 11 column were busy. By October 19, he and Luckman were working together, and many had agreed to be part of a national committee. Pearson was also busily seeding his column with letters of interest he had received: the Lions Club committed to get a car from the Pacific Northwest to Ogden, Utah; Kansans were promising to fill dozens of cars with wheat; Oklahomans were on board; a citizen from Massachusetts suggested that each donation have a nametag including the address of the donor.

But there was a lot left undone, and the availability of a train loomed large. For more than two weeks, as public interest in the Friendship Train grew, Pearson had yet to secure a

---

[7] *Letter and submission to Variety, February 26, 1948. LBJ Library, Drew Pearson Archives, Roxanne Goddard research, document 1930.*
[8] *Interview with the author, August 14, 2018.*

promise from the Association of American Railroads. It was a nail-biting time: Pearson was on the public stage, furiously promoting a train he had no guarantee would exist.

Finally, on October 26, [9] the wait was over. Pearson announced that executives at all five railroads[10] had pledged their support, free of charge: a mile-long freight train would indeed make its way from California to New York Harbor. Pearson had his train; all he had to do was fill it.

8. What to Give

To make sure that what America provided would be needed and welcome in Europe, Pearson borrowed from the Department of Agriculture, which had conducted what is described as an "exhaustive study" [11] to determine European nutrition needs. Pearson sent this list to members of the National Friendship Train Committee who disseminated it to their networks. Then he wrote personally to governors who in turn wrote to mayors, who passed the message on to local

---

[9] *Transcription of Pearson's broadcast on Sunday, October 26: "Last week I reported that Mr. Charles Luckman of the Citizens' Food Committee was seriously considering a train of Friendship to begin in Los Angeles and pick up box cars of food as a dramatic demonstration of American generosity to the people of Western Europe. I can now report the American Association of Railways has graciously agreed to operate such a train. The Presidents of the Southern Pacific, Union Pacific, Northwestern, Pennsylvania, and NY Central did not hesitate a minute and were delighted to put a freight train approximately one mile long at the disposal of the Committee."*

[10] *Originally five railroads were committed to the project, but as the train crossed the country, it grew. The Santa Fe RR joined in Wichita; the Chesapeake and Ohio took over in Washington; the Baltimore and Ohio made a final haul to Philadelphia. Chicago and Pennsylvania lines; and New York Central collected from upstate New York.*

[11] *From "Friendship Train News Bulletin," undated – LBJ Library, Pearson papers, photographed by Roxanne Godsey, Document RG 1919. Points number 6 and 7 discuss the foods needed and the challenge of repackaging.*

organizations. Communities would have little more than a week or two to collect wheat, flour, evaporated milk, dried peas and beans, sugar, macaroni, spaghetti, unscented soap, and other recommended commodities. Individual contributions—packages of macaroni or a few cans of milk—began to add up to hundreds and then thousands of tons of food, which could not be shoved willy-nilly into a freight car. It all had to be repackaged for shipping in bulk.

This repackaging generated logistical challenges at every station, but the Shipping and Storage Branch of the railroads provided specific direction. Volunteers at collection points coordinated with the railroads so that well in advance of the train's arrival, contributions were at the station ready to be put in containers with like goods and loaded on to a waiting boxcar. Since the Friendship Train stopped in each station for just an hour, everyone had a job to do.

Despite the challenges of orchestrating so many people over such distances, Pearson remained upbeat. "For perhaps the first time in history, the average American sees a chance to do something to influence the foreign policy of his country," he crowed in his Merry-Go-Round column on November 8. Food, he went on, was now "just as much an instrument of foreign policy as tanks or battleships. ... in the end, it may mean the difference between peace and war."[12]

---

[12] *Merry-go-Round column dated November 8, 1947.*

9. Ordinary Americans Show Up

The first boxcars of what Pearson hoped would eventually become a mile-long Friendship Train were scheduled to roll out of Los Angeles before midnight on November 7. If Pearson had worried about starting with a bang, he needn't have: in the days before the big kick-off, Californians showed up in droves to donate food. American Legionnaires collected 100-pound sacks of flour; the children of Greenfield Union school in Bakersfield gave up ice cream money to join big Kern County ranchers in buying a carload of wheat. The Teamsters Union sent trucks to pick up donations from scattered communities and further agreed to send crews to stations across the country before the train arrived to help pack boxcars along the way. The promise of the Friendship Train had not only excited and inspired people, it had catalyzed them into action.

By November 1, Pearson wrote that nationwide reaction to the Friendship Train had been so great that, "It now looks as if the chief worry will be whether the railroads and New York harbor will be swamped."[13]

10. A Hollywood Send-Off

Twenty-seven days after Pearson published his October 11 column, the national Friendship Train committee hosted a kick-off extravaganza in Hollywood and it was as ostentatious as Drew Pearson and Committee Chairman Harry Warner, with

---

[13] *Merry-go-Round, November 1, 1947.*

the collective genius of Warner Brothers Studios behind them, could make it.

On November 7, at 8:00 PM, the parade began in Hollywood as boxcars filled with food were pulled by two electric engines, hooked behind the boxcars were flatcars carrying 150 actors who had volunteered to join the train with the full support of the Screen Actors Guild, which had also filled a boxcar with macaroni. Among the stars were Elizabeth Taylor, who was just fifteen-years-old at the time and had recently won the hearts of audiences as the horse-loving teenager in *National Velvet*. Towering over her was the international star of western and war movies, John Wayne. The stunning twenty-seven-year-old, Irish-born American actress, Maureen O'Hara, her auburn hair ablaze in the lights was also aboard. O'Hara had just finished filming what would become a top-grossing Christmas classic, *A Miracle on 34th Street* [14]. Actor, comedian, dancer, singer, songwriter and popular radio host, Eddie Cantor, whose voice was like a family-member in households across America, made for a lively and friendly master of ceremonies.

Cheering spectators lined the streets from La Brea to Vermont to Silverlake Boulevard in Hollywood, waving flags beneath klieg lights that striped the night sky as 192 professional musicians, making up eight bands from Musicians Local 47, wound their way between floats in the parade through Hollywood. One reporter wrote that mothers and fathers walked with their children to the cars filled with food

---

[14] *A Miracle on 34th Street was initially released as The Big Heart.*

bound for Europe, patted them, and walked away. Some of them, no doubt, held their children's hands a little tighter as they recalled what they, as soldiers and nurses, had witnessed in Europe just a few years earlier.

In Hollywood, the air was balmy and the best show in town was one that ordinary American families had made possible. On the stage, Governor Earl Warren[15] congratulated Californians for their support of Europe, encouraged further donations from states across the country and proclaimed the week of November 8 "Friendship Week" in California. Governors across the country echoed that call in their own states. In a speech afterward, Luckman tempered the optimism with a warning. Communists, he said, were aggressively courting Europeans and "...hungry people may trade their love of peace and freedom for a dictator's piece of bread."

Pearson had imagined rivaling the Soviets' pomp and ceremony and, on that night, he succeeded. He had manufactured one of the day's dominant news events and all the hoopla would be caught on film by crews from Warner Brothers and 20th Century Fox. The journey of the Friendship Train crossing the continent would be news in papers across America and like a wind-driven fire, it would create more news. Importantly for Pearson, the Friendship Train's journey would

---

[15] *Governor Earl Warren, a native of Bakersfield, California, and three-term governor, nominated by both Republicans and Democrats, would later become the 14th Chief Justice of the Supreme Court of the US. A photo of Governor and Mrs. Earl Warren at the spectacular send-off of the Friendship Train in Hollywood ran in the Los Angeles Times, Part I, Saturday, November 8, 1947. Page 6.*

also be broadcast in Western Europe as high-quality newsreels narrated in French and Italian by announcers with sonorous voices, were sent to theaters abroad. There could be no question that the parcels of food on this train came with heartfelt wishes from Americans who lined up on city streets and snowy platforms to see the train they had helped load steam ever eastward.

With a brakeman's lantern, at 11 o'clock PM, California Governor Earl Warren signaled "Go" from the stage in Hollywood. Seven miles up the road, in Glendale,[16] the train's whistle blew and the first twelve cars[17] of the Friendship Train rumbled out of the station. No one knew exactly what to expect going forward, but Pearson knew one thing. His decision to initiate the train in Hollywood had been a strategic choice and it had been a good one. If there was one place on the planet that knew the publicity game, it was Hollywood and Pearson hoped the storm of media attention created by the launch would create an avalanche across the country. He had made the Friendship Train into a spectacle people would not want to miss. At least, that's what he hoped.

---

[16] *The grand celebration was in Hollywood, but for logistical reasons, the boxcars were loaded in Glendale. Twelve boxcars were in tow, eight with donations and four to support passengers, including press, and dignitaries.*
[17] *Some accounts suggest that there were eight boxcars. Others say twelve. The discrepancy is likely due to the fact that there were additional cars to accommodate passengers, including sleeping cars, a dining car, and a flatbed that would act as a speakers' platform.*

11. A Call to Action

One of the reasons the kickoff of the Friendship Train was so successful is that Pearson made doing the right thing feel urgent. From the beginning, he had understood that Truman's Citizens Food Committee's campaign was a good idea—but that it lacked action or context. There is no drama in conserving food. Even for a good cause, there's nothing particularly exciting about skipping a meal. Conservation is something done behind the scenes and quietly and many Americans were already depriving themselves. As one writer opined in an editorial letter, Truman's "Save Wheat, Save Meat, Save the Peace" program "caused considerable adverse comment because many of us, due to necessity, have already reduced or eliminated meat, poultry, and eggs from our tables."[18]

Mandatory rationing had ended after the war, but Truman continued to ask Americans to voluntarily limit consuming some commodities like meat, eggs, and grains without explaining why. As Mrs. Kathryn Stone of the League of Women Voters exhorted the food committee, "You've got to tell American women the whole story behind the need for conserving food if you expect them to have the political maturity to cooperate wholeheartedly. You've got to tell them exactly why it is so vital to our own welfare that we help friendly European nations. That hasn't been done."[19]

---

[18] Letter to the LA Times, October 13, 1947 from James E. Potter, 1518-29th Street, Santa Monica, CA. Accessed from Drew Pearson Friendship Train archives, LBJ Library, RG document 1847.
[19] Washington Merry-go-Round, October 13, 1947

People had been roused to do something during the war because war is inherently dramatic. Beginning in late 1942, newsreels, magazines, newspapers, and radio brought stories of troop movements to the big screen and into homes. People saved cans because they could be made into munitions; women who had previously defined themselves as housewives proudly became mechanics and truck drivers; communities grew victory gardens because it would mean more food for the troops. Hunger is quiet, it does not call attention to itself. But in Washington, politicians and government watchdogs like Drew Pearson knew that another war, a cold one, had begun and the battleground was a hungry Europe. As Secretary of State George C. Marshall said, a hungry people will give their allegiance to whomever feeds them.

From Pearson's perspective, the Friendship Train was a message of peace and it did two things: First, it provided motivation to conserve and gave people something to do immediately with what they had quietly saved. It was not a long, drawn-out, save-now-give-later campaign. It was a call to quick action because the train was on its way. Secondly, like the Luckman campaign, he tapped into the nascent fear of another war and suggested that food was the antidote. But again, he took the idea a step further by making the connection from pantry to peace by repeating over and over that Americans had a powerful tool of diplomacy in their kitchens. It was a message people understood. By dramatizing the Friendship Train, Pearson touched that same spirit of patriotism that had motivated the country to initiate the building of a war machine in December 1941.

In his speeches at train stations across the country, Pearson also repeatedly contrasted the freedom of democracy with life under a communist dictator. Stalin did not have to ask permission to take from farmers what they couldn't really afford to give; the State owned their crops, and Stalin had the power to commandeer them.

The seed at the core of Pearson's campaign was that the future of Europe was at stake. If Americans didn't help the western democracies, Europe might embrace communism and be swept under the Iron Curtain. Americans, he exhorted, should not only give what they could to the train, they should show up at the stations to be seen and filmed so that Europeans could see that the food on this train was a gift from ordinary Americans. As J.A. Osborne from Louisville, Kentucky wrote, "If average folk in Europe knew the heart of average folk in America, the ones that bear the sufferings of war, it would take some slick leadership to rouse them to the killing stage."[20] Putting an ordinary face on American diplomacy was exactly what Pearson hoped would come of the train he set in motion that late night in November 1947.

---

[20] *Western Union telegram to Drew Pearson dated October 13, 1947. Accessed from Drew Pearson papers in the LBJ library. RG document 1845.*

Part II. Eleven Days, Eleven States

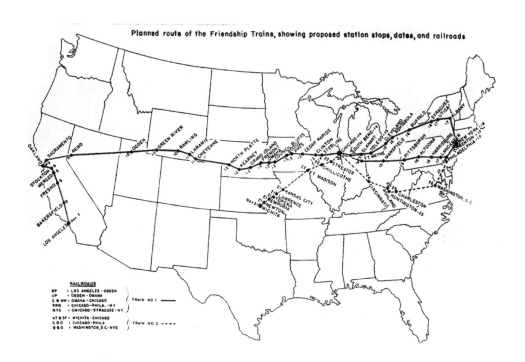

Planned route of the Friendship Trains, showing proposed station stops, dates, and railroads from the Drew Pearson papers, LBJ Library, Austin, Texas.

Day 1: California – Saturday November 8

After its star-studded sendoff in Hollywood on November 7, the train began its journey to the East Coast. The Friendship Train would travel across just eleven states, those that drew the straightest line from California to New York. From Los Angeles, the train headed north through California's Central Valley stopping in Bakersfield, Fresno, Merced, and Stockton. Pearson and his team could not control how much each city would donate, but they could exert some influence over publicity and Harry Warner left nothing to chance. In a detailed memo to all local Friendship Train chairmen, Warner advised local coordinators that there would be a camera crew aboard the train and newsreels would be recorded, edited and sent abroad to show the recipients in Europe how ordinary Americans made this train possible. To enhance the film, therefore, citizens should be on hand to salute the train on arrival. If possible, a parade should be organized from the main street to the station to draw a larger crowd to the station; stores and offices should be closed; and school children should be given permission to welcome the arrival of the train and participate in ceremonies while the locally donated carloads were being added to the ever-lengthening train.

Partly due to the fact that Associated Press photos of the Hollywood sendoff got picked up on front pages across the country, crowds in every town gathered, waving flags, cheering, singing patriotic songs. High school bands played, adults and children patted the train, sometimes adding a chalked note to the side. Stations were decorated and loaded freight cars often sported signs saying: "To the People of France and Italy from the Hearts of their Friends in ...Fresno, Stockton, Oakland, Sacramento..."[21] Sometimes, as in Bakersfield, there were signs in English, French, and Italian. After leaving Los Angeles, every small town with a station and a stop did itself proud with parades and ceremonies and flags waving.

---

[21] *Food from the Friendship Train went not only to France, but to Italy and other western European countries. This story focuses only on France.*

The first big metropolis the train chugged into after its send-off in Hollywood was the port city of Oakland on the San Francisco Bay. The train, now twenty cars long, arrived at 7:45 PM, and the city put on a reception second to none. Roads were closed to accommodate a parade downtown and a crowd that was more than double what it had been in Los Angeles cheered as the train drew into the station and floodlights crisscrossed the sky. A police color guard marched with a motorcycle escort, a dozen high school drill teams, and twenty-six bands paraded down Franklin and Broadway. At Oakland's 16th Street Station, Pearson repeated the phrase that he would use at every stop across the nation: "There's not one Government official aboard and not one cent of Government money was spent for the food."[22]

Pearson had reasons for emphasizing this point: He wanted to frame the difference between communism and democracy. "The Russian wheat came from the Soviet government—not from the Russian people," he wrote in his column on October 11, 1947. "Not more than a handful of Russian people even know about it." The presence of California's governor on the train, and a cabinet member sharing the stage in Hollywood, renders Pearson's statement about no official government involvement imprecise, but it was true in this sense: The train, was given a hearty thumbs up by the White House[23] as its message echoed that of the Citizens Food Committee, but it was neither sponsored nor financially

---

[22] *Warner and Pearson's comments are as cited in the New York Times, "City to Welcome Food Train Today," November 18, 1947, page 1 and 31.*
[23] *Washington Merry-Go-Round, October 27, 1947*

supported by either federal or state governments. And, of course, the train was not something done in secret.

The momentum of the train rolling thousands of miles across the country was generated by people who gave willingly and voluntarily. No one was required to show up to give food, but the Friendship Train was front page news and donating to it gave ordinary citizens a sense that they were part of a team, participating in something bigger than themselves. Collecting supplies for the train that was coming to town became the thing that everyone was doing, separately but together. Maybe they liked Pearson's idea that they were engaged in a form of international diplomacy; maybe they were simply offering friendship to people who had less than they did; maybe people liked the idea that there was no government involvement. Whatever the motivation, the Friendship Train's momentum was created by Americans who gave because they wanted to, not because they were required to.

Hawaii

You cannot take a train to the Hawaiian Islands and, in any event, in 1947, Hawaii was not yet a state. But neither of these conditions prevented the residents of the territory 2500 miles off the coast of California from contributing generously to the Friendship Train and they had a commodity much in demand: sugar.

The logistics were simple because Hawaiian sugarcane was refined in Crockett, California and was already there—it just needed to be paid for. This could have been simple because the Hawaiian sugar industry had agreed to pay for it themselves, but the residents of the islands were insistent: This was a gift from people to people and they wanted to pay for it. On November 1, donation cans appeared wherever people gathered. Newspapers and broadcasters spread word of the campaign: Islanders needed to raise the cost of a boxcar of sugar, $6500 (equivalent to $76,000 in 2019 dollars), and they had just a week to do it. On November 7, Hawaii's Governor Ingram Steinbeck was scheduled to fly to Los Angeles to join the train. If they could raise the money, a boxcar of sugar would be added in Oakland.

In Hawaii, people were encouraged to drop a few cents in the can and they did by the pocketful. With an average donation of eight pennies a person, Hawaii raised $10,884 (about $128,000 today) and the Hawaiian Sugar Planters' Association kicked in the difference for a second boxcar. In Oakland, Governor Steinbeck was elated to find that his constituents had donated not one, but two boxcars to America's message of friendship for Europe. Though not yet a state, Hawaiians had the honor of being the only donor whose contribution crossed two oceans and a continent.

Day 2: Nevada - Sunday, November 9

He knew his state was getting a late start, but on November 1, Governor Vail Pittman made his appeal to Nevadans. The Friendship Train was just eight days away from its only stop in the Silver State and Pittman worried that there wasn't enough time for Nevadans to round up food to fill even a single boxcar. His urgent request was heartfelt. "It is Nevada's obligation to contribute to the Friendship Train. Failure is unthinkable – it would place the great state of Nevada in a very bad light, which would reflect everlasting discredit. Each citizen in responding to this patriotic and humanitarian call will not only be helping to stave off starvation in Europe but will also bring good will for this nation." [24]

Nevada is a vast desert state populated by big ranches and small towns separated by hundreds of miles of arid landscape peppered with sagebrush, but Nevadans were not to be outdone by their glitzy, more populous neighbor to the West. Cub Scouts went door to door in Hawthorne and Babbit; Senior Scouts packed food in Sparks; the fire chief from White Pine County drove a truck 400 miles to get his county's contribution to Reno in time to meet the train. In Yerington, the boys of Future Farmers of America collected food from houses, businesses, and farmers. And school children gathered over a ton of canned and dried food, which was all boxed and labeled by the high school agriculture class. Farmers in Smith Valley donated seven tons of wheat and barley. Residents of Henderson, Boulder City, North Las Vegas and Overton collected three tons of food in several trucks, then kept driving hundreds of miles north and west to collect donations from Tonopah and Hawthorne. A truck from Ely drove three-hundred miles on the old Pony Express route and stopped at collection points in Eureka and Austin. The Lovelock state

---

[24] *"Friendship Train to Gather Food for Europe's Needy, in Reno, Nov. 9."*
Nevada Appeal, November 3, 1947, p. 1

highway department drove two trucks with Pershing county's contribution, and four trucks from Elko made stops in Winnemucca, Battle Mountain, and Golconda. Reno firemen packaged donations from local schools while students from the University of Nevada drove over 700 miles to haul wheat from remote ranches.[25]

On the morning of Sunday, November 9, Governor Pittman flew to Sacramento, California's capital, where he participated in ceremonies with Governor Warren, then boarded the train to cross the Sierras from Sacramento into Nevada. By the time the train rolled into Reno at 7:00 PM that same day, two Nevada freight cars loaded with 126 tons of food were ready for hitching. With a population of just 150,000 compared to California's 10 million plus, Pittman's buttons were bursting, "I am tickled to death at the response the people of Nevada have made to the Friendship Train. Every man, woman and child of Nevada has a right to be proud."

The temperature was well below freezing, and the train would dally just long enough for the four thousand people crowded into the railroad crossing at Center Street to sing "God Bless America," hear a few speeches, applaud the Stewart Indian School band and cheer for the train and themselves. The mayor of Reno crowed that he'd bet a new hat that the people of Nevada gave more per capita than any state in the union.[26] Whether or not the mayor won a new hat can't be known as the

---

[25] Report of Nevada participation for The Mason Valley News, . Friday, November 7, 1947, Page 1.
[26] "Big Sendoff to Friendship Train Given: Thousands Brave Icy Weather to See Ceremony," Nevada State Journal, 11 November 1947, page 14.

speed of the train across the country left little time for tallying, but it is clear that Nevadans had a right to be proud. At 8:00 PM, the locomotive surged to life and with twenty-nine cars in tow, the Friendship Train headed to Utah.

Day 3: Utah – Monday, November 10

Sixteen hours after leaving Reno, the Friendship Train arrived in Ogden, Utah, where Governor Herbert Maw presented his state's contribution: two boxcars loaded with wheat and a third with evaporated milk. The Utah stop was a short one, as the schedule demanded that the train keep moving on the planned route and schedule, but in Utah, something wonderful began to happen: Boxcars from states not on the route that Pearson had planned joined the Friendship Train. In Ogden, a total of six boxcars were added –three from Utah, two from Idaho and one from California that had missed the send-off. The train had crossed through just three states, but already five states and one island territory had contributed.

There is a touch of electricity in the stories surrounding people's efforts to fill a boxcar. Pearson had built on the habits that had been encouraged on the home front during the war by giving people something specific to do. During the war, victory gardens, conservation, eating leftovers, doing without, and rationing had all been part of daily life. In his column on October 27, Pearson wrote, "I was talking to a young lady who said that life was easier during the war...people knew exactly what they should do and did it." By the time the Friendship

Train reached Utah, it was clear that Pearson's idea had tapped into the same spirit of patriotism that had energized the war effort. Given something they could do, people enthusiastically responded.

Of course, contributing states—whether or not they were on the mainline— needed leaders who could inspire people to give on a local level, manage the collection, and coordinate transportation. A good example of that kind of leadership was the Lions Club in Oregon, two states away from the nearest stop, that sponsored a boxcar to be picked up along the route.

Day 4: Wyoming – Tuesday, November 11

In order to power over the Rocky Mountains, the Friendship Train that had begun in California split into two sections. As it climbed more than seven thousand feet above sea level to the pass over the Continental Divide, temperatures dropped, wind rose and snow frosted the windward side, but the train kept chugging, making its way into Wyoming. Its first stop was the little town of Green River, population 2,000, where it was cheered on by the Kemmerer High School band and loaded up with 10,000 pounds of macaroni: five pounds for every man, woman and child in town.

The sun hadn't yet risen when the train pulled into Rawlins the next morning at 4:30 A.M., but within a couple of hours hundreds of local people bundled in woolen winter wear, gathered at the station, stamping their feet in the snow. The local radio station broadcast the event live and by 7:00 AM, high school musicians celebrated the train's arrival and sent it off to its next hundred mile run to Laramie. The train's final stop in Wyoming was Cheyenne, where a delegation from Colorado joined the festivities and 4,000 people gathered to cheer what was now forty-five carloads of food collected from the American West, headed east to the snow-covered flat country of Nebraska. It was the largest crowd in Cheyenne's history.

Day 5: Nebraska—Wednesday, November 12

Five stops were scheduled in Nebraska, but the "cornhuskers" were insistent that in addition to North Platte, Kearney, Grand Island, Fremont and Omaha, the train also needed to stop in Sydney and Lincoln[27], too. At every station, boxcars were added, cameras rolled, speeches were made and bands played, but Pearson would later write that Kearney's was the most exciting early morning jubilation he had ever seen.

Kearney's population in 1947, was around 10,000, and it appears that every organization in town participated in project Friendship: the Kearney Legion Drum and Bugle Corps, Future Farmers, Boy Scouts, veterans from both wars, churches, and schools. At church, in grocery stores, at work and in schools,

---

[27] *Another train that is sometimes confused with the Friendship Train is the "Lincoln Train," also known as the "Lincoln Friendship Train," which originated in Lincoln, Nebraska to commemorate Abraham Lincoln in February 1948. Though the Lincoln Train was not a part of the Friendship Train that Pearson initiated, its mission was similar in that it collected wheat, flour, and milk to send abroad to countries in need. The beneficiaries of the Lincoln Train were Austria, Germany, Poland, Korea and Japan.*

everyone gave pennies or nickels, cans of milk, sacks of flour, or bags of beans. The den mothers of Scout Troop #1 made sure that their neighbors and the crowd gathered at the station knew that the scouts had earned every dime by themselves.

People gave what they could, but John Crom from Aurora also contributed an idea. Crom had been a prisoner of war in Japan and he well remembered how extreme his hunger had been. It was November, and though the Nebraska fields had already been harvested, ears of corn were left to rot scattered across the furrows. Here was waste, he thought. A single ear is not much, but in the fields around Aurora, bushels might be collected, and they could be made into flour. Crom shared his idea with one person, then another, and in the way that things can get done in a small town where people talk to each other, the school principals agreed that it was a worthy project and it was decided that junior and senior high school students could be dismissed early to glean the fields. With the temperature hovering around freezing, students swarmed the fields and bent to the task of picking corn from 1000 acres of American farmland for hundreds of school children in France.

A Special Guest in Omaha

The Friendship Train's last stop in Nebraska on Wednesday afternoon was the capital city of Omaha and Pearson devoted much of his column to the special guest aboard that day: French Ambassador, Henri Bonnet. Some of the people gathered to hear Bonnet speak might have heard him before as he had visited America's heartland during the

Second World War. He was a veteran of WWI, and had endured four years of mud, shelling, terror, silence and the death of comrades on the Western Front. He won the Croix de Guerre (War Cross) for his courage, but having seen the devastation, despair and futility of a war that claimed many friends, scores of countrymen and millions of lives, he began to work with the League of Nations, a body he hoped would end war forever.

But war came again in Bonnet's lifetime and when Germany occupied France in 1940, he escaped to England to become part of the fledgling "Free French Government" headed by Charles de Gaulle. It was de Gaulle who had sent Bonnet to America to do what he could to counteract German propaganda, which was fanning the flames of isolationism. France needed America's support, while clearly Germany needed the U.S. to stay out of the war. De Gaulle sent Bonnet to explain to Americans that the whole idea of "America First" would only serve to help Hitler and the Nazis: free countries are the strongest when they work with, and for, one another.

During Bonnet's prior visit to the U.S., he had learned just how strong the pull of isolationism was in the Midwest. But the idea that America should not intervene in the war against the Axis powers lost traction after Pearl Harbor and by 1947, the U.S. was fully committed to joining and, perhaps even leading, the international community. Bonnet knew, too, that citizens now understood that fighting to end the Nazi regime was morally right.

When Bonnet came to speak from the Friendship Train's flatcar in Omaha, he brought a message of gratitude. It was a heartfelt thank you to America for the gift of their friendship, and for so much more. The war in which so many French and American soldiers died was over, but his homeland continued to be a political battleground. Whether communist or democratic ideals would win out was yet uncertain. On the day Ambassador Bonnet spoke to Nebraskans about the importance of helping the French people through difficult times, the newspaper reported that "the Mayor of Marseille, who had been elected on a De Gaullist ticket, was violently assaulted by communist-led demonstrators."[28]

The Breadbasket Special

Neither Texas nor Oklahoma were on the train's route, but Pearson had arranged for a second train to originate in Wichita, Kansas, which was close enough for big, burly Texas to figure it couldn't be left out. As R.O. Seely from Wortham, Texas wrote to Governor Beauford Jester on November 8, "Texas needs to participate so it would be recognized abroad for its warm heart and sympathetic understanding. ... We believe it is unthinkable that Texas fail to have a share in such a project."

Oklahomans felt the same way so E.N. Puckett, the grain manager in Enid, Oklahoma and the vice-chairman of Oklahoma's Wheat for Relief committee, approached the Santa Fe Railroad. It didn't take the executives long to ponder the request. With the Santa Fe Railroad's help, they could see that the ranches and communities of the Southwest could get

---

[28] *The Ogden Standard Examiner, November 12, 1947, page 1. "Mayor Beaten by Marseille Reds."*

contributions to Kansas. In short order, the Santa Fe Railroad joined the effort, donating 120 cars, each with a capacity of 125,000 pounds. They would be made available without charge so that every little town, club, church or school that wanted to participate could.

Though Texas was not on the original route, enterprising farmers, businesses, civic organizations and churches from the Southwest collected thousands of tons of grain to join the Friendship Train. Photo from the Drew Pearson collection at the LBJ Library.

The geography of the Southwest is defined by vast distances, enormous ranches, rolling prairie grass, piney woods, small towns and big cities separated by hundreds of miles. With freight cars promised, and little time, hundreds of people worked to get their community donations to the nearest station. In quick succession, service clubs, railroad executives, churches and ranches organized. In Texas, the Lions Club was particularly active and before long a web of spurs converged in Fort Worth, for the push to Wichita and east. This network of trains had many names and many points of origin: the Texas Food for Peace Train, the Train of Mercy, the Panhandle Train, the Wheat Train, the Bread Train, and the Breadbasket Special. Together they allowed the Southwest to participate and together they filled every last one of the 120 cars provided by the Santa Fe Railroad to capacity.

Day 6: Iowa—Thursday, November 13

In 1947, syndicated columnist and Iowa native, Marquis Childs, wrote that his state was once the geographical center of what was considered the "Isolationist Middle West." But that label, he wrote, no longer applied. The Iowa Farm Bureau enthusiastically voted to procure a hundred carloads of grain for free distribution in Europe. And twenty-two Iowa farmers traveled to Europe at their own expense, then came home to preach the need for getting food to Europe as quickly as possible. [29] Pearson also debunked the notion that "the Midwest was going isolationist, pulling back into their shell

---

[29] Childs, M. (1947, November 28) Washington Calling: Iowa Farmers Realize Europe Needs U.S. Aid The Arizona Republic, page 6. Retrieved from https://www.newspapers.com/image/116947369/

and saying to heck with Europe—which of course is what Russia wants most."[30] He went on to say that there may be some of that, but people repicking their fields to send grain to Europe and setting up their own wheat relief committees without prompting from Washington, is not isolationism, that's democracy.

Whatever the motivation, Iowa, with a population less than a third of California's, filled at least one freight car at every stop: Council Bluffs, Ames, Boone, Cedar Rapids and Clinton. Every community and surrounding rural area participated, but the city of Ames, not far from the state's capital in Des Moines, made their drive particularly public by erecting a thermometer on Main Street and setting a goal for the town: In eight days, could the citizens of Ames raise $10,000 for food for Europe? Every day the red of the thermometer rose as donations climbed toward the goal. At Ames High School, homerooms competed with each other to bring in the most cans of milk. Eight hundred and ninety cans came in. The contest was repeated at Central Junior High, where 560 cans were added to the stockpile. Meanwhile on Main Street, the thermometer rose until it exploded out the top. In just eight days, Ames had raised $15,780.88, which is more than $178,000 in 2019 dollars, and many thousands more in food. By the time the train crossed the state line into Illinois, it was twenty cars longer than it had been when it rolled in from Nebraska.

---

[30] *Drew Pearson, Washington Merry-go-Round, October 17, 1947. Retrieved from American University Digital Research Archives.*

Day 7: Illinois—Friday, November 14

The Friendship Train made several stops in Illinois, adding twenty-eight cars total, and even though the first stop wasn't the biggest, it seemed to include the entire town of Sterling. Factories blew their whistles to announce the train's arrival so no one would miss it, shops and retail stores put signs in the windows: Closed to welcome the Friendship Train! Schools dismissed their students, and five thousand people, nearly half the population of the town, gathered for an hour to celebrate the Friendship Train.

For the two weeks before the train's arrival, it would have been impossible to be in town and not know the Friendship Train was coming. Journalists wrote about its mission, broadcasters tracked its progress, ministers talked about the needy in Europe, and educators prepared students, teaching them where the train was going and why Europe needed America's help.

When the train arrived that Friday morning, the high school band entertained the crowd and elementary school students wrote their names and traced their hands on the freight car carrying the 68,000 cases of canned milk they had helped to collect. They hadn't personally milked the cows, but they knew where that milk came from and they knew where it was going. Some of their parents and grandparents had been to Europe during one of the wars, some had been born there, and some knew loved ones who had gone there and never came home. All of the children could trace the train's tracks from California right to their town where for one glorious hour that

51

Friday morning, they gave it a flag-waving welcome and a heartfelt sendoff.

Day 8: Chicago—Saturday, November 15

After chugging out of Sterling, the train pushed on to Chicago, which became a hub with several spokes. The train that had started in Los Angeles cruised into the Windy City from the west, then split into two sections going east. The first eastbound line veered north through Indiana and western New York, while the southern line cut straight through Central Ohio and Pennsylvania. A week later, another spoke chugged in from Wichita carrying the bounty of the Breadbasket states and yet another train rumbled out of Chicago headed south then north, picking up Cincinnati, West Virginia, Washington D.C. and Philadelphia.

Classroom by classroom, church by church, and town by town, the trains filled up. As Dorothy Bush, history teacher and international club advisor at the Streator Township High School in north-central Illinois said, the Friendship Train gave students a way to put action to their motto, "Building friendly relations with the world."[31]

Day 9: Ohio – Sunday, November 16

Two branches of the Friendship train crossed Ohio. The northern route included stops in Elkhart, Toledo, Cleveland and Ashtabula, while the southern route stopped in Mansfield.

---

[31] *Story about Dorothy Bush from Streator is from Dorothy R. Scheele's Friendship Train website.*

At every stop there was, as in the rest of the country, a show of patriotism and always Pearson (who was riding on the Mansfield train) or the mayor or the governor or a local dignitary would emphasize the democratic nature of the effort. The Friendship Train was successful because they, the people, had made it successful. At every station there were crowds, music, bands, and posters.

In Cleveland, on Sunday morning, November 16, a young woman from Cincinnati stepped forward on the make-shift stage and smiled a little shyly. The crowd of 3,000 standing in icy rain leaned in. Born twenty-two years earlier in Ohio, Irma Mohaupt had spent most of her life in Europe. She had spent the last two and a half in a Russian labor camp. Her story was harrowing. The previous Tuesday, Irma had stepped off the S.S *Marine Flasher* in New York to freedom. It was front page news. Her father had been murdered by Russian communists; her mother remained where they had last lived together in Yugoslavia. But Irma was the most blessed: she was in America again. In Russia, she said, "people are told that in America, there is no food, no clothes. They are told that they are lucky to be in Russia. The propaganda is everywhere, but no one believes it; no one has enough food. And, of course, there is no freedom."[32]

That the Friendship Train was a show of what a free people living in a democracy could do was a point made over and over by Pearson. He continually repeated that the

---

[32] *Irma Mohaupt's whole story has been recorded by Jody McKim Pharr on the Danube Swabian History website.*

Friendship Train could not happen in the Soviet Union and had begun his campaign with that idea when he compared how the U.S.S.R. and the U.S. were helping Europe. "The Russian wheat came direct from the Soviet government—not from the Russian people. Not more than a handful of Russian people even know about it. The American wheat, on the other hand, was saved and collected after a mass campaign by all the American people in which farmers shipped wheat early and every housewife cut down on her use of bread."[33] With clergy and business people and media personalities on the platform with Mohaupt, hundreds of children waved flags and the forty-piece band of professional musicians played the national anthems of France, Italy, and America.

Day 10: Pennsylvania – Monday, November 17

On Monday, November 17, the top story in *The Evening News* in Harrisburg, Pennsylvania, began with the sentence: "Two of the greatest post-war symbols of democracy in action, the Freedom Train and the Friendship Train, met in Harrisburg this morning amid historic ceremonies that were broadcast to the world."[34]

These two celebrity trains were, indeed, tributes to democracy, but they had very different missions. While the Friendship Train carried nourishment and encouragement to Europe, the Freedom Train, which was traversing the country

---

[33] *Washington Merry-Go-Round column, October 11, 1947.*
[34] *"Friendship and Freedom Trains' Paths Cross Here First and Only Time." The Evening News, Harrisburg, Pennsylvania, page 1. Accessed December 1, 2018.*

between 1947 and 1949, carried the founding documents of U.S. democracy, including the Declaration of Independence, the Constitution, and the Bill of Rights to every state in the Union. The train also carried a recent document, signed by the sitting president: The Truman Doctrine established for the first time that the United States would involve itself in foreign conflicts, it would come to the defense of democracies being threatened by authoritarian nations.[35] In other words, if the communist eastern bloc countries became a threat to Western Europe, the US would not retreat to isolationism.

Another document making the cross-country tour on the Freedom Train was the one that President Abraham Lincoln signed on January 1, 1863. The Emancipation Proclamation changed the nature of America's Civil War from one about preserving the union, to one about granting equal rights for people of all races. That war was long since over, but ideological battles were still being fought. When local authorities in Memphis, Tennessee and Birmingham, Alabama insisted on separating viewers of the Freedom Train by race, the conservative American Heritage Foundation canceled the train's visits to those cities. The U.S. armed forces remained segregated until July 26, 1948, but in many cities, leaders were taking a stand against racism.

---

[35] *With the Truman Doctrine, President Harry S. Truman established that the United States would provide political, military and economic assistance to all democratic nations under threat from external or internal authoritarian forces. The Truman Doctrine effectively reoriented U.S. foreign policy, away from its usual stance of withdrawal from regional conflicts not directly involving the United States, to one of possible intervention in faraway conflicts. From "Milestones in the History of U.S. Foreign Relations" previously maintained by the US Office of the historian.*

With the cost of war so fresh in people's memories, the Truman administration launched the Freedom Train to remind Americans just how hard-won freedom is. The nuclear age had dawned, and the Soviets were reaching into countries American soldiers had just helped liberate from fascist oppression. The Friendship Train in many ways carried a similar message. Every parcel on the train had a label that read: "All races and creeds make up the vast melting pot of America, and in a democratic and Christian spirit of good will toward men, we, the American people, have worked together to bring this food to your doorsteps, hoping that it will tide you over until your own fields are again rich and abundant with crops."

In Harrisburg, people lined up by the busloads and the line snaked between the two trains. If the Friendship Train was democracy in action, the Freedom Train was democracy on parade.

Day 10: (continued): New Jersey – Monday, November 17

On November 17, the day the Friendship Train made its only stop in New Jersey, the front page of the New Brunswick *Daily Home News* was a patchwork of contrasts. Top stories were about Truman's call for sacrifices with rationing and wage ceilings, and just below it is a photo of volunteers loading 176 cases of food on the Friendship Train, "as a gift to destitute Europe." Meanwhile at the United Nations, Andrei Y. Vishinsky, the Soviet Deputy Foreign Minister and chief Russian delegate raged that Americans were pitting Germany against Russia and that in America "there is a frenzied ideological upsurge of public opinion in favor of war with the Soviet Union."[36] On the same page, headlines noted that communist-initiated strikes were threatening to paralyze France and Marseille was already incapacitated. As volunteers loaded a freight car in New Jersey, 30,000 coal miners in France joined striking transportation and dock workers in solidarity.

None of this news stopped the New Jersey volunteers who had a deadline to meet. The contributions from their state had to join two more trains converging in New York Harbor the next day.

Day 11: New York – Tuesday, November 18

Eleven days after the initial sendoff by tens of thousands of well-wishers in Los Angeles, hundreds of thousands of people gathered in New York to join the Friendship Train festivities at its final US destination. As trains from north and south and west converged in New York, the total number of cars had yet to be tallied, but as the train of friendship crossed the country, it was clear that the idea had become contagious.

One Friendship Train had become many Friendship Trains, all bearing thousands and thousands of tons of commodities. It was not as long as Pearson had hoped; it was far, far longer. Getting that many tons of goods unloaded, repackaged, then packaged again in larger containers, and strapped in the hold of a ship would amount to a job of staggering proportions. It

---

[36] *"Vishinsky Says Public Opinion Favors USSR War: Soviet Minister is Principal Speaker at Dinner in New York," The Millville Daily, (New Jersey), 17 November 1947, page 1.*

would be nearly impossible to do so in time to cross the Atlantic and chug from the north to the south of France by Christmas. But that was a problem for another day.

First, as the trains chugged in, it was time to celebrate. Fire boats sprayed a confetti of droplets against the blue sky and a cacophony of boat horns, whistles, and cheers rose from the Hudson as barges carrying thirty-three Friendship boxcars that had traveled all the way from California circumnavigated New York Harbor. The barge took the Friendship boxcars past France's earlier gift to the U.S.: the Statue of Liberty, which was given to the United States in 1886 to celebrate the alliance of two countries since the American Revolution. A crowd that police estimated to number 100,000 lined Lower Broadway for a parade that began in the Battery and marched up Broadway amid flurries of torn paper drifting from high buildings.

The parade included contingents of police, fire, and sanitation departments, marchers of French and Italian descent in national costumes, Boy Scouts and Girl Scouts and, of course, marching bands. [37] At City Hall 25,000 people had gathered to hear speeches. Three of them were given by American children who spoke in English, French, and Italian. Then, in a shortwave broadcast directly from France, the crowd heard a child's high voice crackle over the radio, thanking America for the food it was sending to French children.

On Tuesday, November 18, just eleven days after eight boxcars left Los Angeles, *The New York Times* reported that 270

---

[37] *From the New York Times archives, November 18, 1947, page 1+. Accessed from timesmachine.nytimes.com.*

boxcars converged in New York from Weehawken, West Side and Greenville yards, Jersey City and Philadelphia. More trains would follow and nearly seventy years later, archived reports of the total number of cars in the Friendship caravan vary wildly. According to Pearson's reporting, the train on the route that had originated in Los Angeles accounts for a total of 225 cars; the train that came through Wichita and collected the Breadbasket States accounts for another 270 cars. As Pearson carefully notes, this total of 495 cars did not include 17 carloads of bulk grain that had been dropped off to be milled into flour in Philadelphia. In addition to the approximately 500 cars that made their way in two main sections across the country, 164 boxcars were added by charitable organizations. These donations from groups like the Mennonite Central Committee and the Christian Rural overseas program were not officially part of the collection motivated by the Friendship Train, but they were permitted to join the train on its final leg to benefit from free railroad transportation to New York and Philadelphia.[38]

New York finally tipped the Friendship Train's total tally with an outpouring of donations that would have filled 25-30 freight cars, but these donations were trucked directly to Pier 42 and were never on a train. The grand total, if you count all the donations, was likely around 700. The train Drew Pearson dreamed to fill was a mile long. With the average 1940s freight

---

[38] *The number of boxcars coming into New York from several points are from the official Friendship Train report archived in the Drew Pearson papers at the LBJ Library. (RG #1856)*

car between forty and fifty feet long, the trains that Americans actually filled would measure, end to end, nearly six miles.[39]

While the exact number of boxcars is elusive, an accounting of cars is less important than the fact that in November 1947, millions of Americans chose to give something of themselves to people they would never meet. Across the country, Americans had stood shivering in the late autumn chill in town after town, waving and cheering, singing patriotic songs, and chalking messages of goodwill on boxcars that would travel thousands of miles. They had given spaghetti and sugar, dried peas and beans, but mostly they managed to load a ship with good will, a commodity that is without weight or dimension, but priceless nevertheless.

12: Harbor Preparations

After the parades in the city, came the work at the dock and by every measure, the work that lay ahead was staggering. Over a quarter of a million units—cartons, drums, and bags— collected from across the country had to be unloaded from the train, packaged, insulated, and then loaded and strapped for shipping across the ocean in the hold of the ship. The logistics of labeling alone were complicated as every package had to be marked. Goods that had been collected and wrapped by countless volunteers across the country had to be sorted. Steamship companies donated space and stevedoring.

---

[39] *Average 1940s train sizes provided by Wendell Huffman, Nevada State Railroad Museum.*

But Christmas was just five weeks away and it would take nearly three of those weeks to cross the Atlantic and transit France. It was clear by the end of November that everything could not be ready by the planned sailing date. The final report on the train in Pearson's papers was explicit. Not all donations could be loaded and shipped at once. In fact, even loading vessels would take over a month. Records of the New York Office of the Shipping and Storage Branch say that "for thirty-four days between December 7, 1947 and January 11, 1948, crews that numbered from twenty to 102 men worked daily, nights, Saturdays, Sundays and even Thanksgiving. Normal working hours went by the wayside as shifts worked around the clock." [40] America's permanent delegate to the United Nations called the work they were doing "peace mongering."

Originally just one ship was scheduled to take the train's cargo to France, but when the newly christened *Friend Ship* was unable to carry all eleven million pounds, three more ships—the *American Banker, De Grasse*, and S. S. *Chinois*—were added with crossings scheduled later in December and early 1948. There were also worries that even if American ships made it to France, the food would languish on board. In France, throughout fall and winter of 1947, dock strikes had left cargo in ships and transit strikes had left hundreds of workers stranded. Whether or not the cargo that had been so joyfully collected across America would be unloaded in Le Havre in time for Christmas remained a question.

---

[40] *These numbers and dates are from the final report on the Friendship Train in the Drew Pearson Archives, LBJ Library. RG document #1864.*

But by early December, with so many obstacles overcome already, the American people forged ahead. On December 7, 1947—less than two months after Pearson published that fateful column—the *Friend Ship* steamed out of New York Harbor laden with the first 3,913 tons of American gifts.

Part III. The Friendship Train in France:
Le Train de l'Amitié Américaine

1. Gabrielle Griswold – An American in Paris

Gabrielle Griswold had just turned twenty-one when she moved to Paris in the summer of 1947. Before the war, she had spent a year in France, attending a French school where she "was the only foreigner, the only non-Catholic, and (God forbid!) the only left-hander!"[41] In high school, she was a student at the Lycée on the Upper East Side in Manhattan. She was fluent in English and French, and had excellent secretarial skills, which she honed as a volunteer at the offices of American Aid to France (AAtF). In the New York office, Gabrielle had assisted personnel who were collecting food, clothing and medical supplies for shipment to Paris; at the AAtF headquarters in Paris she would replace the outgoing receptionist and provide administrative support on the distribution end.

Seventy years later, Gabrielle remembers that her parents were supportive, but the letters she has saved and neatly catalogued, also remind her how much they worried. France was at peace, but Communists were agitating, and general strikes were common. In June 1947, Gabrielle set sail with her French godmother, Marie-Louise Fontaine, on the *S.S. America* from New York to Le Havre. Marie-Louise had arranged for Gabrielle to rent a narrow room, "not much wider than the

---

[41] *From an email from Gabrielle Griswold to the author, February 8, 2018.*

door," in St. Mandé, a Paris suburb at the end of the Metro Line #1. The apartment was airy in summer and frigid in winter, but on those first summer mornings Gabrielle remembers a delightful cacophony: behind her building the lions of the zoo at Saint Vincennes roared above the roosters in the gardens below. She remembers that, "In those lean years, nearly everyone who had a small garden raised chickens or rabbits to supplement meager rations."

At work, Gabrielle was the most bilingual of the staff and she thrived, soon distinguishing herself as intelligent, able, and industrious. During the summer and early fall of 1947, she often took her noontime break at the "Etoile" where there was a public swimming pool. But in mid-October, an unexpected responsibility accelerated the pace and there were no more breaks: Drew Pearson had designated AAtF to distribute resources collected by the Friendship Train.

Robert Blake, the director of AAtF in Paris was a former banker and an able administrator. When Pearson talked to him about adding the Friendship Train to his distribution network, Pearson wanted to be clear about what he was asking him to do. But the truth is, in late October, Pearson couldn't have known how much the American people would give. He was asking Blake to take on a task of unknown proportions with a firm deadline: a portion of whatever arrived must be distributed throughout France by Christmas with as much publicity as Blake and his team could muster.

The task, amorphous as it was, would require coordinating many agencies and Blake immediately reassigned his twenty-one-year-old bilingual receptionist, file clerk, and part-time secretary, Gabrielle, to another role: full-time secretary for the Friendship Train, which was renamed in French "Train de l'Amitié." In late October, a riot erupted in Paris, and though this was no direct threat to Gabrielle, by the end of November she was so busy working days and nights, she had no time to correspond with her parents. In a December 18 letter, her mother wrote, "I have no recent news of Gabs. They tell me that mails from France have been extremely slow and that a lot of the mail was lost. But it is now almost four weeks since I have had a letter from her, and I am very much worried. She's probably all right, but it's natural, with all the unrest over there, and the cold houses, sickness, etc., that I should be uneasy."

Seventy years later, Gabrielle remembered this time with joy and disbelief. How so many people came together to do so much in such a short time was nothing short of remarkable.

2. American Aid to France (AAtF)

Americans had swarmed the beaches of Normandy on June 6, 1944, and a month later, on July 5, American Relief for France was incorporated to provide relief for the people whose cities and towns were destroyed in the process of liberating the

On D-Day, 73,000 American forces joined Allied troops who landed on the beaches of Normandy. Precise numbers are not available, but an estimated 2500 Americans died that day in France, mostly on Omaha Beach. During the Normandy campaign, 15-20,000 French civilians died, most were from Allied bombs. Photo by author May 2018.

country. Two years later, its name was changed to American Aid to France and their obligation was defined as "representing America in its expression of good will to the people of France on the basis of meeting immediate needs for relief supplies and also of establishing a continuing relationship in matters of relief, rehabilitation, and welfare." [42] In France, the organization worked with a network of religious groups and distribution agencies to get supplies where they were needed.

In 1947, when Gabrielle joined AAtF staff in Paris, the offices were on the fourth floor of Pershing Hall, just a few blocks from the Arc de Triomphe. General John J. Pershing never used the hall for his base of operations, but the building was dedicated to him after World War I as he built the American forces from 130,000 men to over two million and helped turn the tide in favor of the Allies. Gabrielle well remembered Pershing Hall as it was in 1947:

"At street level, GIs and many Americans gathered. To the left of the front doorway there was a soda fountain-cum-snack bar that served ice cream in dishes or cones, sodas, shakes, sandwiches, and other goodies. Just past the soda fountain, was an open courtyard on the left, and just beyond that, still on the left was a bar, which was open most of the day and into the evening. The fact that Pershing Hall was known to contain so many Americans made it an occasional target for beggars. I especially remember one: a late-middle-aged barefoot woman in rags, who hung out beside the front door, soliciting money from anyone who entered or left the building. Despite the fact that some French colleagues warned me that she appeared to them to be very much a fake, I had seen her swollen, red, and

[42] *From the AAtF 1946 Handbook. New York Public Library archives – Box 1, accessed by the author in February 2018.*

roughened feet, so I took pity on her and did sometimes disburse a few coins into her outstretched hand.

"In the street, one did, not infrequently, encounter beggars whose 'wartime' injuries or poverty might or might not have been as real as they pictured them to be. It was hard to distinguish the real from the fake, so I always rather felt that, to be on the right side, one ought to be generous rather than parsimonious, and although I too was living on a shoestring, I could usually spare a small amount. Besides beggars, of course there were street singers and musicians, and sometimes music wafted up to our top-story windows from a radio or record player and treated us to the latest popular American songs or older classics— welcome sounds, that cheered us while we worked." [43]

And work they did—long days and late nights. Gabrielle remembers that working as the secretary of the Friendship Train was interesting and fulfilling and required understanding where there was the greatest need. But it also required understanding and navigating the deep fissures that divided the nation. The divisions were political, to be sure, but they were also religious. Jews, Catholics, and Protestants all had to have a seat at the friendship table as allocation and distribution was planned. Plans had to be made and coordinated with the French Ministry of Public Heath, the U.S. Embassy, Entr'Aide Française, and the Croix Rouge Française

---

[43] *Personal correspondence with the author, February 21, 2018.*

(French Red Cross) because without buy-in from these key groups at the outset, success could be compromised, and the sought-after publicity could well be negative. Every one of those organizations wanted to serve all who needed it, but it is also true that each group had a vested interest in making sure that members of their particular constituency were not left out and compromise, even among those who seek to do well, is sometimes elusive.

3. France – November 20, 1947

As America was pulling together, France was tearing itself apart. There was plenty of work to do as whole cities needed to be rebuilt, but there was no money to pay for what needed to be done. Many were homeless and disabled. There was not enough coal to heat apartments or petrol to drive a car, so commutes were done mostly by metro, bicycles and tricycles. Gabrielle recalled the cold:

"In Mademoiselle Sasse's otherwise unheated Saint-Mandé apartment, there was only one heating unit, at mid-point of the long central hallway. During the cold winter of 1947-1948, I believe that she only turned it on twice on two especially cold weekend afternoons, when she, Mlle. Troupel and I sat around it on chairs to enjoy its heat for perhaps half-an-hour— warming the front of our bodies, which of course remained un-warmed in back, as the unit's heat made little impact on the long hallway's icy air. The apartment was usually so cold that I remember writing

amusedly to my mother that I could actually see my

breath in the air even as I was writing her."[44]

In the fall of 1947, as the Friendship Train was being paraded and loaded into ships in New York, riots rocked Paris. Socialist Premier Paul Ramadier had resigned, communist leaders called for a strike and 500,000 coal miners, metal workers, longshoremen, flour millers and railway workers walked off their jobs. Paris teachers threatened to join, bringing all civil servants with them in solidarity. President Auriol responded by appealing for calm while simultaneously recalling 140,000 conscripts to bring the army up to "normal strength."[45]

Tension in France was high. The country had just emerged from a catastrophic war and soldiers were again making their presence known in the streets. For five years, France had been divided physically and politically between the Nazi-occupied territory in the north and the collaborationist Vichy government in the south and the scars of that division had not had time to heal. The French Resistance had a nominal leader in De Gaulle, but after Hitler invaded the Soviet Union, the bulk of the resistance movement in France had been fueled by communists, giving them a strong postwar foothold. Both the U.S.S.R. and the U.S. were viewed as allies who had liberated them, but both were also viewed with some suspicion by different factions. From the East, Stalin was understood to be

[44] *Correspondence from Gabrielle Griswold with the author, February 6, 2018.*
[45] *New York Daily News, 21 Nov. 1947, page 610. Accessed from newspapers.com September 16, 2018.*

making a power grab, as the previously occupied countries of Bulgaria, Romania, Hungary, Poland, parts of Czechoslovakia and Eastern Germany already had lost their sovereignty to become Soviet satellites. From the West, the United States was seen by many as imperialist, though its reach was not for territory, but for markets that would support a capitalist economy.[46]

In 1947, when U.S. Secretary of State Marshall first proposed his European economic recovery program, popularly known as the Marshall Plan, communist hardliners in France encouraged by the Soviet Union mobilized against it, insisting that it was a capitalist move that would, in the end, mostly benefit the U.S. Others argued that the plan was a viable lifeline that would allow France and Europe, but not the Soviet bloc, to recover, rebuild, and unite Europe.

It was into this political climate that the Friendship Train and its thousands of tons of donations, entered. Of course, the Friendship Train was not directly related to the Marshall Plan in any way, but they shared thematic similarities, and the overwhelming and enthusiastic public enthusiasm for the train may have encouraged some senators to support the Marshall Plan in Congress. As Warren Austin, U.S. permanent delegate to the United Nations, said to the crowd that had gathered at City Hall to welcome the train in New York on November 18, the

---

[46] *Only one organization conducted public opinion polls at the time. In a survey taken at the USSR's high point, just after the Paris liberation, 63% of the population said that the country that contributed most to German defeat was the USSR. Only 29% believed the US did. To the question "What is the most important problem you and your family must currently face? 53% of those surveyed responded "replenishment," a word that was used to include "bread" or "meat." In 1946, a quarter of the population believed that both the USSR and the USA were imperialist.*

many gifts to the Friendship Train "should leave no doubt that the policy of the government is the policy of the people."[47]

Even as the *Friend Ship* prepared to sail, the politics in France remained murky. Pearson worried that prolonged dock strikes, and a politically divisive climate could undermine what he perceived to be the diplomatic mission of the train. In his vision, the people of France needed to welcome the American gifts with open arms. But that was far from guaranteed. If there was a strike, or the donations never made it to French families, all would be lost. Pearson tapped David Karr, his executive assistant, and charged him with the formidable task of averting such a disaster.

4. The Advance Man

David Karr is an interesting character. As a young man, he wrote for the Communist Party publication, the *Daily Worker*, and earned a penny-a-line for his efforts. He then moved on to a job in the U.S. Office of War Information (OWI). Called to testify before the House Special Committee on Un-American Activities, Karr fabricated a story that he was working for the FBI, when in fact he was reporting to the KGB,[48] a fact that was

---

[47] *"City Hails Friendship Train: Food Total is Put at 270 Cars." New York Times, November 19, 1947.*

[48] *In Fortune magazine, December 3, 1979, Roy Rowan wrote, "By the time Karr was twenty-five, he had worked as a Fuller Brush man, New York Daily Mirror reporter, penny-a-line writer for the Communist Daily Worker, investigator for the Council against Nazi Propaganda, employee in the Office of War Information (where he was let go after being called before Martin Dies's House Un-American Activities Committee), and star legman for Washington columnist Drew Pearson. Digging up dirt for Pearson surely sharpened Karr's cloak-and-dagger instincts." Accessed from http://digitalcollections.library.cmu.edu/awweb/awarchive?type=file&item=590 263*

substantiated by official records after the Soviet Union collapsed decades later. He left the OWI on his own accord, if under a bit of a cloud and was snapped up by Pearson. No matter the circumstances of his leaving the government, the stories Karr could glean from his extensive network inside the government could help Pearson with the daily feeding of the *Washington Merry-go-Round.*

In November 1947, Pearson sent Karr to France to make sure that everything went smoothly on that side of the Atlantic. Karr received an official and warm welcome from the French government, the American Ambassador, and American relief agencies. Exactly what David Karr did unofficially remains off the record, but logic suggests that between his arrival in France in late November and the docking of the ship in the harbor, he was able to do something that the French government had been unable to do.

Gabrielle Griswold (2nd from right) is taking minutes at a Friendship Train Steering Committee Meeting with representatives of French and American charitable organizations. Robert Blake, director of the American Aid to France office in Paris, is far right.

5. Paris - December 12

Beginning in late November, the Friendship Train Steering Committee met almost daily in Blake's Office in Pershing Hall. Correspondence grew and special stationery was printed in English and French: American Friendship Train Committee—

Comité du Train D'Amitié Franco-Américaine. The *Friend Ship* was mid-Atlantic when Blake convened the committee of eighteen to finalize distribution plans. Representatives from the French Ministry of Public Health, the U.S. Embassy, YMCA, Church World Services, National Catholic Welfare Committee, Sisters of Saint Vincent de Paul, Entr'Aide Française, and the Red Cross made a layered semi-circle facing Blake at his desk, flanked by his assistant, Florence Gillian, and Friendship Train secretary, Gabrielle Griswold, who took notes. David Karr, was also present.

The challenge facing the group was, by all measures, a good one to have. They now expected that the *Friend Ship* would dock on December 17, at Le Havre and it would be carrying nearly four thousand tons of foodstuffs that needed to be allocated. The steering committee already had met several times to identify to whom and where the goods would be distributed. At the December 10 meeting, the unanimous agreement had been that the bulk of the food should go to children through school cafeterias, while some percentage should go to the elderly. All distributions would be in cities, not suburban or rural areas. Now that they had more information about the amount of food that would be available and less than a week before the ship's arrival, they needed to confirm the details of their action plan. At five o'clock, Mr. Fanon from the French Ministry of Public Health set the tone: There was not enough for everyone. Whatever they decided had to be clear to the public, able to reach destinations rapidly, and subject to the least amount of criticism.

The committee worked well into the night, but eventually all participants agreed to confirm the decision they had made unanimously on December 10, to focus on young children because "it was preferable to do a greater amount of good among a small group than a small amount of good among a great many groups."[49] Eight percent of the distributions would go to homes for the Elderly, which provided meals, but not lodging to those in need. The bulk of the food would go to children in select cities that were hard hit by the war, with almost half of the cargo—47%— staying in Paris and the nearby metropolitan area, known as the "Département de la Seine." There would be no attempt to get what could only amount to meager amounts to suburban and rural areas beyond city limits.

Supply lines were complex and the black market robust. All the charity groups knew that despite their best efforts, it was possible, even likely, that some of the food meant to be given for free could be stolen and sold. To minimize the possibility of black marketeers selling Friendship gifts, the committee agreed that the food would be consumed as a "goûters", or supplemental nutrition break, by only those children who ate in the school cafeterias, a discrete group that the minister of public health identified as most needy. Serving the food at school, would minimize the ever-present danger of it being collected and sold illegally by unauthorized middlemen.

---

[49] *Minutes of the Friendship Committee meeting on December 12, 1947, 5:00 PM. From the Gabrielle Griswold Collection.*

As they allocated specific percentages to thirty-three cities that were working hard to rebuild from the war's devastation, all the agencies involved hoped that every pound would get to where it was most needed. The committee's plan was detailed and well thought-out, but not everything worked out quite as they had planned.

6. Select Cities

On December 13, the Steering Committee finalized the cities that would be on the Friendship Train route and the percentage of the supplies that each city would be allocated.[50] The challenge of dividing and distributing a shipment that had been spontaneously given and collected often with little regard for the guidelines, was enormous. While the original recommendations provided by the U.S. Department of Agriculture listed only nineteen goods, many collection points were not so strict. Canned vegetables or jars of maple syrup were not supposed to be included in the collection, but in America, not all small donors, particularly those who were far from collection points, were familiar with the rules. As their bulk and weight made them impractical to ship such a distance, some of their good intentions were left at train stations or on the dock in New York for distribution in America. Still, in the end and even with diligent sorting at collection points, seventy-

---

[50] *The committee planned to distribute Friendship food to thirty-three cities:Lille, Rouraix, Tourcoing, Arras, Calais, Boulogne, Dunkerque; Nancy, Metz, Strasbourg, Mulhouse, Saint-Die, Montbeliard; Marseille, Toulon, Avignon, Montpellier, Nice; Lyon Saint Etienne, Grenoble, Dijon, and Valence, Rouen, Le Havre, Nantes, Saint-Nazaire,Toulouse, Brest and Lorient, Bordeaux, Paris and Seine.*

one different varieties of food products made their way to France. Much of it was happily enjoyed by school children and the elderly, but some goods that had journeyed thousands of miles on land and sea, were in the warehouse in France, where they would meet with a different fate.

The S.S. American Leader was rechristened the "Friendship" for this special voyage from New York to France. This newspaper clipping says "Moving messenger of American solidarity towards France. The Friendship loaded with 500 wagons is warmly welcomed in Le Havre. [Note that the ship was not carrying actual wagons or boxcars, but it did carry nearly 4000 tons of cargo that had been collected in the trains that crossed America.] Photo from the Gabrielle Griswold collection.

7. Le Havre – December 17, 1947

Pearson knew that the political situation in France was dicey, and it wasn't just the dock strikes and the communist agitation. As the Friendship Train was crossing America and its cargo was being stowed to sail to France, French newspapers were peppered with stories of civil unrest and protests. On some occasions, the anger was directed at the U.S.'s proposed Marshall Plan. Just five days before the *Friend Ship* sailed from New York Harbor, radical labor activists sabotaged a rail line in Paris and sixteen people died; fifty others were injured.

While Pearson had taken great care to separate the grassroots Friendship movement from the American government and its plans to help Europe with a formal recovery program, the political climate was ripe. As the *Friend Ship* steamed into Le Havre harbor, where the dock was crowded with dignitaries, families, and the press, many worried that anti-American communist agitators would use the occasion to cause a scene. In the communist press, nothing at all was written about the *Friend Ship*'s arrival in Le Havre as they chose not to amplify its message by giving it any media coverage.

Months later, a Russian journalist would opine that the Friendship Train had been "filled with chewing gum, socks and hairpins and was quite comparable to the boats full of penknives that Hitler sent to Germany's satellites in an effort to win their allegiance,"[51] but the gathering in Le Havre was

---

[51] *Description of the contents of the train was published in the communist newspaper, Litteratournia Gazeta, on March 31, 1948. Contemporaneous records disprove this claim.*

peaceful. There was no riot, no slow-down, no disruption of any kind. It's possible that the communist leadership decided on their own not to disrupt the arrival of food which they, and their countrymen, desperately needed. Maybe they thought that a strike against this particular shipment would generate negative publicity for them and positive press for America.

It's also possible that, given his bona fides within leftist circles, David Karr might have had some rapport with communist leaders. Though it's speculation, this mutual understanding might have generated a backroom deal. Surely, it's extraordinary that dock workers that had, as recently as November, paralyzed the port, opted to work without pay. As Pearson wrote, "In the end, the dock workers of Le Havre, whose strikes previously had crippled that Communist-dominated port, volunteered to unload the *Friendship* without pay. After they had finished, we gave them one ton of food for their children. But they did not know this gift was forthcoming when they offered to work free."[52]

That last sentence reads like an afterthought, though it may be true. Documentation shows that the steering committee authorized this gratuity at the December 20 meeting, which was attended by both Drew Pearson and his assistant, David Karr. Whether or not palms were greased or promises made before that meeting, we don't know, but Pearson's advance man certainly delivered on his mission to

---

[52] *From the LBJ Library, Drew Pearson collection: European Friendship Train Report. (RG doc 1944)*

get the Friendship Train's contents safely to shore in a timely manner.

In Le Havre, speeches were given by the American Ambassador, Jefferey Caffery and by the Minster of Public Health and Population, Germaine Poinso-Chapuis, who was a lawyer from Marseille, a recipient of the Medal of Resistance, and the first woman to be appointed to a Cabinet-level position in France. Representing all the agencies that were involved in the distribution, Robert Blake, director of the Friendship Train in France, told the assembled audience that his task was both joyous and serious. Joyous because many ordinary Americans – school children and businesses, railroads and farmers and many more had joined together to send these goods to France. Grave because it is a heavy responsibility to distribute these gifts when there is so much need. Every region has suffered, he said, yet it is our task to choose who receives help.[53] He enumerated the cities where the food would be distributed and that the primary recipients would be children.

With what their friends in America gave, he said, the children of France will know a less harsh winter and happier holidays. "This food sent by people of good will represents the hearts of Americans." Even as Blake spoke first in English for the foreign press, then in more detail in French, the

---

[53] *Blake's speech provided a geographical outline of where the Train of Friendship would travel: from Le Havre to Rouen; Paris and surrounding suburbs; Lyon and nearby cities; Lille and cities in the North of France; Strasbourg, Metz, and certain other cities in the East. In the south and west, the train would reach Bordeaux, Toulouse, Brest and Lorient, Marseille and St.Nazaire.*

dockworkers began the task of hoisting crate after crate from the hold of the ship to the docks where trucks waited.

While her boss was welcoming the train in Le Havre, Gabrielle was in Paris transcribing notes into formal minutes that would become American Aid to France's official record of what happened to America's gifts after they arrived. The months of preparation were about to be implemented and though she did not yet know it, Griswold would be rewarded for her many long days and late nights. Representatives of several groups were scheduled to take a ceremonial journey by train from Paris to Marseille and one of them had just canceled. The new lineup of representatives included three religious organizations. Their names as recorded in the minutes were: Mr. Norris from the Catholic organization; Mr. Schiffer from the Jewish organization; and Miss Griswold who, in addition to her secretarial duties, would represent the Protestant organization.

Trucks draped with American flags and posters were loaded with Friendship food in Le Havre for a ceremonial parade in Paris then on to urban centers throughout France. It was the first time in peace time that trucks were allowed on the Champ-Élysées. Photo courtesy of the LBJ Library, Drew Pearson Archive.

8. Paris – December 19

Two days after the *Friend Ship* docked in Le Havre, Robert Blake convened a publicity meeting that included representatives from AAtF, the International YMCA, the U.S.

Embassy, Church World Service, and the Joint Distribution Services who brought along two publicists.[54] Mr. Malamuth, who directed the publicity arm of the Joint Distribution Committee, advised the group that five hundred pounds of leaflets, printed in French by *Look* magazine, were already winging their way on a T.W.A. flight from New York. At midnight, they would be trucked to the train station, the Gare St. Lazare, and the Hotel de Ville, where the Mayor's office was located, in time for the day's ceremonies. Four publicity points were enumerated: 1) The Friendship Train was strictly a private, people-to-people gesture from the population of the United States to the population of France; 2) it was a thoroughly spontaneous idea that grew overnight to reach the proportions that it did; 3) it is totally non-sectarian in nature; 4) speakers were advised to point out the non-official character of the food distribution.

The official photographer sought to understand the purpose of the pictures he would be taking and the group agreed that the primary objective was as a record of sequential events, copies of which would go to each of four voluntary agencies who were paying for the photographer's work: American Aid to France, the National Catholic Welfare Committee, the American Joint Distribution Committee, and the Protestant Church World Service. Though photos were not

---

[54] *As Friendship Train secretary one of Gabrielle's tasks was recording notes for committee meetings, which she shared with the author in 2018. The December 19 meeting included: Mr. Blake, Miss Griswold (AAtF), Mr. Lowrie (International Y.M.C.A.), Mr. Schneider (U.S. Embassy), Mr. Pitzer (Church World Service), and Mr. Malamuth, Mr. Taylor (photographer) and Mr. Duteil (Joint Distribution Service)*

intended to supplement the French press, who would have their own photographers, the committee believed that the more publicity the train generated, the better, so wider distribution of the photos was welcome. Unfortunately, not all publicity turned out to be good for the fate of America's gifts.

9. Dissension—December 20

It took ten days for dissension to emerge on the steering committee. On December 10, the committee had unanimously agreed on a plan. On December 12, the plan was confirmed. A week later, the representative from the National Catholic Welfare Committee threatened to withdraw from participation if his organization's concerns were not addressed. By limiting distribution to children in cafeterias, Norris complained, too many needy children were left out. Besides, he argued, students who could eat in the cafeteria were actually better off than those who couldn't.

Norris's concern had to be addressed, but the morning was already crowded with events as hundreds of spectators and dozens of dignitaries welcomed a thirty-six-car freight train drawn by an American-made locomotive as it streamed in from Le Havre to the Gare St. Lazare in Paris. Transport Minister Christian Pineau, U.S. Ambassador Jefferson Caffery, Drew Pearson, and Geoffrey Parsons, editor of the International Herald Tribune, were among those crowded onto the platform along with the entire Friendship Train Committee.

An evening program was also scheduled, but the committee needed to address the possible withdrawal of the

National Catholic Welfare Committee so Blake sandwiched an afternoon meeting between ceremonies. In addition to Norris, who had lodged the complaint on behalf of the Catholics, Blake invited the Minister of Public Health and representatives from three of the agencies charged with distribution: The Y.M.C.A, the Croix Rouge and Entr'Aide Française. Pearson and Karr also attended and for their benefit the rationale for the decision was reviewed in detail.

The ministry was there to support the original decision with statistics and the distribution agencies added the weight of their experience in the field. There were hours of discussion, point and counterpoint, which Gabrielle summarized in five pages of typed, single-spaced minutes. The meeting ended with a small concession to Norris and the Catholics: School directors were authorized to allocate some of their supplies to needy students who were not receiving cafeteria meals, but for the most part, distribution would proceed as planned.

Drew Pearson (4th from left in light colored coat) at the Gare St. Lazare, greeting the arrival of the French train bringing Friendship Train merchandise from Le Havre to Paris. Gabrielle Griswold (2nd from left) is next to Robert Blake. Photo from the Gabrielle Griswold Collection.

10. Pearson's Letter to President Auriol

Drew Pearson's December 20 syndicated column published in hundreds of newspapers across the United States was reminiscent of the October 11 column, when he first suggested the idea of a Friendship Train. This time, Pearson's column was again an open letter, but not to Charles Luckman, the chairman of the Citizens Food Committee. Pearson's column was addressed to Vincent Jules Auriol, the President of France.

In it, Pearson explained that the train came into existence because many "plain Americans" felt Congress was moving too slowly to help Europe so they took matters into their own hands. He acknowledges the contributions of businesses, railroads, unions, and farmers and pays particular attention to the stories of a few individuals who represented thousands. The purpose of the column was to give credit where it was due, but also to once again clearly and absolutely separate the train from the U.S. government.

As further proof that the Friendship Train was not government inspired or sponsored, Pearson aimed a gibe at Washington D.C, noting that it was about the only city that did almost nothing to help the Friendship Train, rescued only at the last moment by a local Lions Club. Making it more personal, he added a somewhat gratuitous slur of President Truman who had been in Philadelphia for a football game but did not linger to see a ship sail from Philadelphia with its cargo of food destined for Le Havre. However, he opined, perhaps what he characterized as a presidential snub was for the best because this food, he insisted, came directly from the American people and had nothing to do with the government.

11. An evening in Paris – December 21

Trucks normally were not allowed on the Champs Élysées, but on Saturday Evening, December 20, for the first time in peacetime history, a caravan of fifty French army trucks [55] bedecked with American and French flags side by side, paraded in front of flag-waving crowds down the Champs Élysées, past the Arc de Triumph, onto the Rue de Rivoli to the Hotel de Ville, where Mayor Pierre De Gaulle (Charles De Gaulle's brother) welcomed them.

In the evening, Drew Pearson, assorted dignitaries, and representatives of the American charitable organizations, including Gabrielle Griswold boarded the "Train de l'Amitié." It was to be a trip Gabrielle would never forget. Her memories, supported by dozens of photographs, tell the story of the ceremonial train's journey from Paris to Marseille. Photos taken by the *Herald Tribune* and photographers hired by the Joint Distribution Committee testify to the size of the crowds. With a flag-waving farewell in Paris, the train rolled south to Dijon. Griswold, the youngest member of the group and the secretary of the Friendship Train, recorded her recollections of the Train de l'Amitié's journey from Paris through Dijon and Lyon to Marseille.

---

[55] *The caption on the back of this Acme photo by Rene Henry, Staff Correspondent reads: "Waving American flags, children of Paris cheer wildly at official ceremonies in connection with the arrival of 2,000 [stet] trucks bringing to the French capital part of the cargo of the Friendship Train. Thousands of Parisians turned out for the ceremonies held at the Hotel de Ville (City Hall), December 20th". The number 2000 is undoubtedly wildly inflated. Coverage in the French newspaper indicates there were 50 trucks. Image RG 2279 from the Drew Pearson Archive, LBJ Library.*

School children greet the trucks bearing some of the bounty of the Friendship Train at the Hotel de Ville in Paris on December 20, 1947. Photo by Rene Henry, Acme Photo, from the Drew Pearson archive, LBJ Library.

12. From Paris to Marseille – by Gabrielle Griswold

Dijon – December 22 - morning

For three days, we rode the Friendship Train, stopping at two cities each day, until the third day when we ended our journey at Marseille. Everywhere we stopped, hundreds of people thronged the station platforms to greet us. The train provided by the French government included a dining car, sleeping cars, and several freight cars loaded with a token amount of the Friendship cargo that would be decoupled and left at ceremonies at each stop. Between the living cars and the freight cars, a flatbed became a stage.

Each day aboard the Train began with breakfast in the dining car, during which Blake and I reviewed the short speeches he would make in that day's tours. When the train stopped in mid-morning, we all emerged from inside the train onto the flatbed car. There, Pearson, Blake, welcoming French officials, responding Americans and others addressed the crowd, after which the rest of us in the train's contingent were introduced, stepping forward to take our individual bows-to cheers, applause and much flag-waving from the assembled French people on the station platform below.

These public outdoor ceremonies were then followed by another official welcome elsewhere, either inside the train station or at some more formal vin d'honneur or town hall reception, all liberally punctuated with additional speeches and champagne toasts. While we were being fêted, that town's token boxcar was detached from the train, its contents to be distributed later. When the ceremonies were over, the Train resumed its progress, to repeat the program that afternoon in the next city.

DIJON ACCLAME
le «TRAIN DE L'AMITIE»
cadeau de Noël du peuple
américain aux enfants de France
Un wagon symbolique
« qui sera bientôt suivi de beaucoup d'autres »
a été détaché en gare
Bourgogne Républicaine

Headline in Paris newspaper, "Dijon acclaims the "Friendship Train" Christmas gift of the American people to the children of France. A symbolic car that will soon be followed by many others was detached at the station." Gabrielle Griswold Collection.

Lyon – December 22 – afternoon

The grandest event to which we were treated was at Lyon, where the mayor and members of the municipal council entertained us and a vast company of guests at a lavish banquet, served at what seemed like a mile-long table, in a beautiful, historic hall-the French no doubt having pooled all their ration books, coupons and special allotments to honor us. The food was spectacular, the wine flowed freely, and the whole ambiance was elegant and dazzling, almost like a royal affair. Evening ran into night, speeches were made, glasses raised to Franco-American amity, after which we all made our way back to the train, replete, replenished-and rather weary.

Marseille- December 24

By the time we reached Marseille, it was mid-morning of December 24th, Christmas Eve, and I was exhausted from the excitement, the long hours, the early risings, the consumption of rich food and alcohol—to which at the age of twenty-one, I was definitely not accustomed!

After that morning's vin d'honneur at the town hall, we remained in Marseille for some while, probably going on to luncheon somewhere afterwards. In late-afternoon some of us departed via what chanced to be my first-ever airplane flight, chartered especially for our party courtesy of Air France. That night, we were back in Paris.

For the next month, Blake and I attended several food distributions at schools and orphanages in the metropolitan area, kept up with the paperwork, and prepared to oversee the bulk of the distributions throughout France as the rest of the merchandise arrived from the United States. [56]

---

[56] *This story is copyrighted by Gabrielle Griswold and is recorded here with permission.*

13. Valence and Avignon – December 23

Although Gabrielle's summary does not include details about the stops on December 23, the first in Valence, the second in Avignon, they were greeted with similar, though considerably less opulent receptions. Drew Pearson wrote that he thought they had stayed too long in Lyon and Gabrielle recalled that some of the group stayed not on the train, but in a hotel that night in Lyon. In Valence, Pearson noted that four communist strikers had been killed at the railroad station a few weeks before the train arrived. Communist members of the city council came to the reception anyway. As the mayor told him, the Friendship Train was too popular to stay away.

14 A Light Meal

While Gabrielle was enjoying the ceremonial ride, other spurs of the French railway were disbursing friendship supplies to areas designated in the plan. Each hub had a railway station and from the station, aid workers moved the food to the sites that had been carefully selected.

During the month of January 1948, photos were taken at school sites showing children enjoying a little something extra, which was made possible by the American train donations. The trucks that delivered the Friendship goods from each railway station were well marked so that there could be no mistake where the food came from and these, too, were photographed.

On January 8, in Paris the steering committee discussed several points, including additional tonnage allocated for emergency distributions to the cities of Epinal, Nancy,

Mulhouse, Verdun, and Metz, all of which had been flooded by winter storms. In some locations, the Red Cross found a surplus of baby food, so distribution centers were altered, allowing the Red Cross to use surplus food in their infant food program, which was well established. There appeared to be a sixty to hundred-ton discrepancy between the amount that was supposed to be on the *Friend Ship* and the amount that actually did arrive, but this shortfall would be made up by the arrival of the S.S. *American Banker,* which was carrying 1000 tons and the S.S. *De Grasse*, with 500 more tons. The last ship associated with the train, the *S.S. Indo-Chinois,* would add more provisions in February.

On January 14, 1948, at the AAtF office in New York, the situation in France was summarized for the Board of Directors: Milk production was down by 40% limiting consumption to children under four; grain crops were 25% of what was necessary making it necessary to ration bread to 200 grams per person per day, which amounts to about two or three slices, depending on density. On the bright side, infant mortality and tuberculosis were on the decrease, providing a nutritional supplement for school children had proved vital in raising health levels, and the Director of Overseas Relief Activities and Services reported on the "extraordinary success of the Friendship Train and the efficient distribution operations through Robert Blake's committee."[57]

---

[57] *From AAtF archives in the New York Public Library, Box 2, Exhibit C from the Board of Directors meeting, January 14, 1948.*

Children from an orphanage gather as the truck arrives. The poster says: Nourishment offered spontaneously to the people of France by the people of America as a symbol of their affection. Friendship food was distributed and consumed at schools to ensure it was received by the children.

The "goûters," the traditional French small meal that children or old people received from the Friendship Train might be criticized as being too small to matter, but the truth was the gifts were more than nutritional. A cookie made with sugar from Hawaii and flour from Texas was a personal message from Americans. The cargo carried by four ships across the ocean would not last long, but the message to Europeans from Americans was clear: You are not invisible.

15. Catastrophe

Arsonists destroyed much of the supplies collected over months by American Aid to France and nearly all the Friendship cargo destined for the Paris region was reduced to ash. Communists were blamed. This article was cut from Le Parisien by Gabrielle Griswold in 1948 when she was working as Robert Blake's assistant on the Friendship Train project. The headline reads, "Catastrophe. Fire in the warehouses of Entr'Aide Française." From the Gabrielle Griswold Collection.

On January 30, at 5:15 PM, Drew Pearson received a telegram: "Early that morning in Paris, 30,000 tons of food were destroyed by fire in the warehouse at Bercy. Gifts of food from the USA, Canada, Ireland, and Sweden were destroyed, along with the contents of seven box cars from the S.S. *Indo Chinois* were lost. Fire started on three sides of the warehouse and phone lines were cut. Blake thinks it is arson but does not want to be quoted."

The police later confirmed what was obvious: it was arson. And the telegram was correct in that much had been destroyed, but the cargo of the S.S. *Indo Chinois* was not lost. That ship was still at sea.

Leon Pearson, Drew's brother, wrote that the fire had destroyed "practically all the food destined for the Paris area since distribution began only Wednesday." Exactly how many of the burned tons belonged to the Friendship Train was not clear at the time. Later, Blake reported that only 20 percent of the Friendship Train's donations were reduced to ashes. The other 80 percent had not been in the warehouse and had arrived at intended distribution points.

But while the Friendship Train had lost some commodities, Entr'Aide Française, American Aid to France and other distribution and aid groups lost months of work, and a warehouse, which at the time of the fire was crammed to overflowing with donations that had taken months to generate. As Blake took great pains to explain in a long letter to Pearson dated February 22, one could not look at the disaster without considering the larger picture. The warehouse had been fuller than usual at the time of the fire for a couple of reasons: the dock strikes and the Friendship Train.

The dock strikes in late 1947 had caused thousands of cases to be piled up in various ports; they were just beginning to move from the docks to the warehouse when the Friendship Train arrived in mid-December. Partly because of the train's Christmas deadline and partly because of the amount of publicity the train had already generated, moving the Friendship cargo took precedence. Sorting and packaging for regional deliveries 71 different varieties of food products severely taxed facilities and staff, so for more than a month all other American Aid distribution was held up. As a consequence of directing all labor to the task of expediting Friendship Train commodities, the AAtF lost thousands of cases which ordinarily would have long since gone out but remained in the warehouse to be destroyed by fire.

Though he never said it publicly at the time, it would not be surprising for Blake to wonder if the publicity the Friendship Train had invited had led directly to the warehouse disaster. An article published on January 29, in *Le Figaro*, featured him ceremoniously opening the warehouse gates to admit the Entr'Aide trucks, which were being used to bring the food to the cities identified by the committee. With this symbolic gesture, he inadvertently revealed the precise location and the state of security of the overflowing facility in which supplies were stuffed. Would-be communist saboteurs would have learned a fairly simple way they could undermine this very public American effort. All they needed was the cover of darkness and a few matches. Destroying the warehouse and its contents, however, did not accomplish what the saboteurs hoped. It turned out that, as Blake wrote in a lengthy letter to Pearson, "the fire itself was a blow to communistic influence and thousands of French who might never have benefitted from any of the food, were filled with indignation and took a more personal interest, when confronted by the fact of such wanton destruction."[58]

16. Keep on Carrying On

After the fire, Blake was clearly disheartened that so much hard work had come to nothing. He ended his February 22 letter to Pearson by saying how much this has affected him. Thousands of tons of food, clothing, medicine and equipment were reduced to ashes and though they could be replaced with other shipments, the stuff that had been collected by AAtF over many months was gone and workers were discouraged. Their work simply disappeared, partly because normal distributions were delayed by the very abnormal, but stupendously popular Friendship Train.

Then in his letter, Blake does something astonishing: He asks Pearson himself to tell the workers he's sorry. "I know also of the hundreds and even thousands of American Aid to France workers who cannot help but be horribly discouraged when weeks and months of conscientious and unceasing efforts have gone up in smoke. I can't tell them how sorry I am though possibly you can? If they are not told and not made to realize

---

[58] *This excerpt is from a five-page letter, dated February 22, 1948, from Robert Blake to Drew Pearson from the Gabrielle Griswold archives.*

that it is necessary to do even more, then whoever is responsible for the fire has accomplished his or their purpose."

What Blake did not say outright is what the warehouse guard said to him: If there hadn't been a Friendship Train, the warehouse would still be standing. There are no records to say that Pearson addressed the workers directly, but he did personally raise $40,000 for AAtF. In columns he assured everyone that the spirit of friendship continued to grow as the train had generated a certain momentum that could not be destroyed by fire. France could expect more soon. California was sending the S.S. *Golden Bear* with 400 tons of milk, scheduled to arrive in Marseille on March 2. The Junior Chambers of commerce in Michigan had initiated a "Friendship Caravan" and seventeen cities had joined; from Lincoln, Nebraska, the "Abraham Lincoln Friendship Train" was on its way; and the Rotary Clubs of Maine had loaded a French fishing trawler with seventy tons of food for French fishermen and their families.

Eventually there would be insurance money, though according to French law it wouldn't cover the losses because a warehouse could only be insured to a maximum figure, which is set by an official insurance syndicate. The Entr'Aide warehouse, where all the AAtF shipments including those on the Friendship Train were stored, was valued for insurance at 450 million francs. Because the warehouse was full to overflowing, this represents just 30 to 40% of the total value of goods that were lost; Friendship Train losses alone were estimated by the AAtF to be 404,445,450 million francs. [59] Whatever the dollar amount, the Friendship Train's itemized list of losses includes nearly a million and a half pounds of milk, an equal amount of flour, and 164,000 pounds of sugar. These had all turned to ash and could not be recovered even if some replacement funds were made immediately available, for the simple reason that in France there was no milk, no flour, no sugar available to purchase.

17. Focus on Children

On February 18, 1948, the AAtF reported that 411 tons of American Friendship food delivered by the steamship *Indo-Chinois*, replaced some of what was lost in the fire and was being distributed to school children in Paris and its surrounding communities. This tonnage was initially allocated to old people's and children's homes but was reassigned to the children who had been deprived because of the fire. Instead of receiving nine kilos—20 pounds—each child received three kilos—just 7.5 pounds. But it was something more than nothing and the effect of this decision was positive.

Since the arrival of the *Friend Ship* in December, three additional ships carrying food from the Friendship Train had been sent, and 750,000 school children in designated cities throughout France had received more than five million

---

[59] *This figure comes from the 7 June 1948, document prepared by Louis Clamaron, Directeur du Service de l'Importation, and Gabrielle Griswold, AAtF secretary. The document lists Friendship Train losses in categories and value in francs. From the Gabrielle Griswold archives.*

pounds[60] of nourishment. The final distribution took place on Friday, February 20, at two schools in Paris: one at 5 rue Milton; the other 29 Ave Pierre Grenier. Transportation for the press was made available at the AAtF offices.

On February 21, in the *Paris Herald,* an awkwardly staged photo shows Jefferson Caffery, the U.S. Ambassador to France, looming along with the Prefect of the Seine Department and the President of the Paris Municipal Council above two boys enjoying a special meal with "French dishes supplemented by American food items." The menu included asparagus, beans, and applesauce from the U.S.A.

18. A Hospital Built on Ruins

The town of St. Lô is located in Normandy, less than thirty miles as the crow flies from Utah Beach, where the Allies landed on June 6, 1944. The city had fallen to the Germans in 1940 and four years later, on D-Day, the Americans began bombarding St. Lô as it was located at a strategic crossroads, vital to the Germans for getting supplies to the front. To warn residents, leaflets were dropped, but high winds blew them downwind and many of the bombs fell on residents who had no idea what was coming. Innocent civilians, prisoners of war, and French patriots were all killed by American bombs.

The Battle for St. Lô would last forty-three days and cost 100,000 lives. Major Tom Howie, commander of the 3[d]

---

[60] *Amount recorded in contemporaneous document filed February 18, 1948, by the Friendship Trian Committee in Paris, was 2,284,705 kilograms, which is equivalent to 5,026,351 pounds. Document accessed Drew Pearson Archives, LBJ Library, RG doc #1875.*

Battalion, was charged with liberating the town. On their way to St. Lô, he led his men in the liberation of the 2d Battalion, which had been decimated, was surrounded by Germans and nearly out of ammunition and food. In an effort to liberate the men, Howie himself took out two machine gun nests, then left the 2d with supplies, and pressed on, reassuring his men with the phrase, "See you in St. Lô!"

Major Thomas D. Howie never made it to St. Lô. Killed by shrapnel the day before victory, Howie's men placed their beloved major's body on a lead jeep so that even in death, he would meet them in St. Lô. Draped with an American flag, he was laid on the rubble of Holy Cross Church, where a monument to those who liberated the town now stands. When the battle was over, ninety-five percent of the buildings in St. Lô were reduced to ruins, the cost in human lives was huge, but the German lines had been breached. The Allies had a path to Berlin.

The destruction at St. Lô was immortalized by the playwright, Samuel Beckett, who volunteered with the Irish Red Cross to work in the Irish hospital there. Though Beckett minimized his service in the Resistance as "boy scout stuff," he wrote about his experience in St. Lô in a piece of factual reportage, "The Capital of Ruins." Written for a radio broadcast that never aired, Beckett writes with haunting minimalism. "Accidents are frequent. Masonry falls when least expected, children play with detonators and demining continues." In Beckett's view, St. Lô is a scene of devastation, but also, relentlessly, of hope and perseverance.

Four years after St. Lô was destroyed, Robert Blake suggested to Pearson that insurance money received after the warehouse fire could be well spent helping to build a children's hospital in the city that had been, to use Beckett's words, "bombed out of existence in one night." It would, Blake wrote, "be a permanent memorial of Franco-American participation in a place that represents what was probably the most important battle of the war."[61] After several letters and many months, Pearson agreed.

Communist saboteurs had reduced the size of the Friendship food given to children and old people in the Paris area, but in the end, their loss contributed to building a much more permanent memorial – a hospital for children in St. Lô.

19 From Friendship to Gratitude

By May 27, 1948, the journey of the Friendship Train was officially complete. French President Auriol conferred the Médaille de la Reconnaissance Française, on the members of the Friendship committee as well as those who worked with the AAtF to distribute the friendship food in the field. In the same letter in which Blake had reiterated his suggestion that insurance money go to St. Lô, Blake told Pearson about a train of thanks in the planning process in France. "I am sure that you have heard of the 'Train de la Reconnaissance Française au Peuple Américain,'[62] which is being organized by a number of

---

[61] *Letter Robert Blake to Drew Pearson, May 24, 1948. Drew Pearson papers, LBJ library, RG #1882-3.*
[62] *Translates to "Gratitude Train for the People of America."*

groups in an effort to show the appreciation of the French people for American aid, both voluntary and governmental, which has been sent here during the past few years."[63]

This "Merci Train" has been inextricably linked to the Friendship Train, but as Blake wrote explicitly in his letter, the train from France was a thank you for much more. Thousands of individuals, scores of church and charitable organizations, and the U.S. government had routinely and for years sent packages—small and large, but none was as large as what the U.S. government had authorized the previous month.

On April 3, 1948, President Truman signed into law the "Economic Cooperation Act of 1948"—better known as the "Marshall Plan"—which had been overwhelmingly passed by the 80th Congress. The Marshall Plan paved the way for between $12 to $13 billion U.S. dollars to be funneled to Western Europe to rebuild industrial and agricultural production, establish financial stability, and expand trade. The Friendship Train's role in convincing the legislators to pass this massive bill cannot be accurately measured. But there can be no doubt that the train that crossed the continent rallied ordinary Americans to support relief for people across the ocean who were in need of their friendship.

---

[63] *Letter Blake to Pearson dated May 26, 1948, cited above.*

Children and the elderly welcomed the "Train de l'Amitié" on its ceremonial journey from Paris to Marseilles. Supplies were carried on trains without charge to metropolitan areas throughout France. Two months after the last of the Friendship gifts were distributed, the Marshall Plan was approved by the U.S. Congress. Photo: Gabrielle Griswold Collection

BOOK TWO – MERCI TRAIN

In February 1948, fourteen months after the *Friend Ship* arrived in Le Havre bearing the gifts of the Friendship Train, the people of France sent a returning ship—this one representing their gratitude—back to America. The French Train, officially called "Le Train de la Reconnaissance

Française," became known in the U.S. as the "Merci Train." It was forty-nine boxcars in length. Every car was filled with over a thousand gifts that were to be given to Americans in each of the forty-eight states; the 49th car was destined to be shared by Washington D.C. and the Territory of Hawaii.

While the freight cars of the original Friendship Train had not crossed the ocean, the boxcars of the Merci Train did. They were intended to become memorials to commemorate America's contribution to victory in both World Wars. American soldiers who had been deployed throughout France would recognize these cars. They carried prisoners of war to camps and men to and from battle and were called "40&8" because they could transport either forty men or eight horses. In America, the narrative that is oft-told is that this train of gratitude was France's answer to the Friendship Train.

This reading is true, but only partly. The timing of this gesture of gratitude and a letter written to the Minister of Public Works and Transportation suggest that the Merci Train was catalyzed by the Friendship Train. But it is also true that while the bounty of the Friendship Train was received by very few people, mostly children in specifically targeted cities, the gifts on the Merci Train came from people of all ages in cities and towns, villages and countryside. The selection of gifts that have been collected and preserved in museums across the country tell a bigger story—one of a people who wanted to remember, commemorate, and honor not just the Friendship Train, but many events of a long-shared history.

1. The Original Idea

The idea for the Merci Train began with men who had served side by side with Americans in two wars: Louis Cast, a veteran of both world wars, and André Picard, a veteran of WWII. The men were, respectively, president and general delegate of the National Federation of Veterans and Victims of War of the Railways and the Union of France.[64] The title of the organization is a mouthful, but crucial because it links two groups: the railways and the veterans. On December 18, 1947, the day after the *Friend Ship* docked in Le Havre, Cast and Picard wrote a letter to the minister of Public Works and Transportation. The letter suggests that as France has received America's "Train of Friendship so heavily loaded with gifts and affection, France must respond with a gift that is worthy of France, and also worthy of those who, twice in a quarter century shed their blood for the liberating and safeguarding of France's brilliance." [65] Cast and Picard go on to suggest that veterans and railway personnel are ideally situated to handle the logistical realities of undertaking such a symbolic task that would respond to the American train with a "Train of French Gratitude to the American People."[66]

Their initial plan, like Pearson's original conception for the Friendship Train, was both modest and audacious: Trains would travel on every line through France, collecting

---

[64] *Féderation Nationale des Anciens Combattants et Victimes de Guerre des Chemins de Fer de France et de L'Union Française*
[65] *The Cast/Picard letter was provided and translated by Alexis Muller, researcher and curator of the Merci Train Facebook page.*
[66] *In French: "Le Train de la Reconnaissance Française au Peuple Américain."*

characteristic examples of art, industry and regional production. These gifts would be carefully selected, typically French, and precious – so as to be worthy of an exhibition in, say, New York. After the exhibition, which would honor French culture, they suggested that these valuable gifts could be auctioned, and the proceeds given to the orphans of American veterans. This idea would, he writes, "show America the measure of France's gratitude while strengthening the position of France in the eyes of America."

As part of their proposal, Cast and Picard also suggested that forty-eight American Legionnaires should be hosted on a trip to France, where they would ceremoniously accept the gifts on behalf of their states, which they would, in turn, formally give to their respective governors upon their return to the U.S. How and to whom the gifts would be distributed was left to the discretion of each governor.

Neither the trip for Legionnaires, nor any auctions became part of the final plan, but this letter, the earliest known document about the idea of a "Gratitude Train," both links and differentiates the two trains that crossed the ocean. They are linked by timing, as surely the arrival of the Friendship Train catalyzed a response. But they are also differentiated in content and presentation. The Americans did not send the train itself, they sent foodstuffs. For the French, an important part of the gift was the boxcars themselves, which had historic value, particularly for veterans. Filling these boxcar memorials with gifts from ordinary French people rather than precious items, was not part of the initial plan. That idea was incorporated into the plan some time in spring, 1948.

2. From Idea to Reality

Drew Pearson had no part in initiating or planning the Merci Train, but the idea to express gratitude to America seemed to be in the zeitgeist as more than one group thought about launching a similar project. In early May 1948, Georges Henri Martin, a journalist for *France-soir*, wrote to Pearson to tell him that "Groups of young French people (office workers, students, etc.) have decided to arrange for a 'train of gratitude' from France to America..."[67]

When he replied to the French journalist on May 12, 1948, Pearson was gracious, but not encouraging: "I have been giving more than a little consideration to the proposed French 'Train of Gratitude.' It is a very thoughtful and touching gesture, and I hesitate to say anything that might discourage it. ... Nevertheless, I must remind you that to organize anything like a 'French Friendship Train,' or even a French exhibit designed to travel through the United States, would be a gigantic task..." He goes on to explain that such a train would be difficult or impossible to achieve despite the success of the American Friendship Train and used as an example the "Freedom Train" that had toured the country with America's founding documents. That train, he said, took a full two years to organize.

---

[67] *Letter from Georges Henri Martin, dated May 4, 1948, was sent from the New York office (50 E. 72nd St.) of France-soir and is in the Drew Pearson papers collection of the LBJ Library in Austin, TX. [RG:1980]*

Pearson's reservations about the viability of the train may have dampened the spirits of the youth, but the veterans' group, spearheaded by Cast and Picard, proceeded on an entirely French schedule, which is a little hard to track from this distance in time and space. By spring 1948, Picard was already in the process of collecting available boxcars. Originally designed to transport cattle, then to transport prisoners, soldiers or beasts depending on the war or the front, these battered boxcars, which were all built in France and were the property of the P.L.M.,[68] were meant to be elegantly wrapped packages that would become monuments in each state. In summer, the board of directors of the Association of American Railroads sent a letter to J.B. Verlot, an official of the French National Railroads. In the letter, the board assured Verlot that all American Railroads were on board to support the project; Merci boxcars would be delivered to all forty-eight states without charge.

The veterans' and railroad men's idea was in motion and Pearson, despite the reservations he had expressed to the journalist about the idea of a train of gratitude, agreed to help Picard and Cast with their project. This was not an easy task as there were many problems to be solved stateside, not the least of which was that American law required that goods coming

---

[68] *P.L.M. stands for the origin and destination of the train: Paris á Lyon et á la Méditerranée. In a letter from the French Ambassador's office, dated February 23, 1949, Arnauld Wapler, Counselor in the Office of the French Ambassador to the United States, Wapler wrote that "it is true that some freight cars of the type 8/40 have been built in Middletown for the French Railroads. Nevertheless, all the cars of the Merci Train are French built and were the property of the former P.L.M. Company. From the Drew Pearson collection in the LBJ Library, document RG 2033.*

into America must be taxed. How in the world would these gifts be valued? Who would pay taxes on forty-nine refurbished, but nevertheless old, boxcars? What about the boxcars' contents? Finally, and most importantly, how would a destitute France pay any taxes at all to the American government? There was only one way around the taxation issue: The 80th Congress, had to pass a bill granting an exception for the Merci Train and all its gifts. To help solve this problem, Drew Pearson, with his network of connections in Washington D.C., was ideally situated.

3. The "Do Nothing Congress" Does Something

The 80th Congress was predominantly Republican and clashed frequently with President Harry S. Truman, the Democrat in the White House, who dubbed the legislative branch, the "Do Nothing Congress." This nickname was not quite fair because the 80th Congress in fact passed several hundred bills including, in April 1948, the massive Marshall Plan, which began the infusion of billions of American dollars into struggling democracies in western Europe. That France's coffers were being filled with American dollars was not lost on either Republicans or Democrats in Congress.

If Congress failed to introduce and pass a bill that got the Merci Train and its contents around the existing legislation, the U.S. essentially would be taking back dollars in taxes they had just given in aid. Republican Senators Robert A. Taft of Ohio and Eugene Milliken of Colorado teamed with Democratic Representatives Sam Rayburn of Texas and Aime Forand of

Rhode Island to provide bilateral leadership. Joint Resolution 433 passed without dissent on June 25, 1948; President Truman signed the bill without comment; and resolution 433 became Public Law 769.

Public Law 769 gave customs officials the authority to allow the Merci Train and everything in it, whatever that might be, to enter the United States duty-free. All fees, charges, and taxes were to be waived.[69] The thousands of packages would not be opened; the boxcars would not be searched. The only restriction was that the resolution would expire on December 31, 1948.

In mid-October, the plan continued to be that a ship or ships that had not yet been located would be loaded with forty-nine boxcars that had not yet been refurbished and filled with assorted gifts that had not yet been given. This ship would arrive in New York on December 17, one year to the day after the *Friend Ship* had arrived in Le Havre. If the ship sailed on time, the deadline attached to Joint Resolution 433 would not

---

[69] *H.J. Resolution 433 (Public Law 769) Resolved by the Senate and House of Representatives of the United States of America in Congress assembled, That any articles, including approximately forty-eight railroad cars and incidental equipment, certified by the Secretary of State as being donated in promotion of international good will by the people or Government of the Republic of France for sale for charitable purposes in the United States or for presentation, in the case of the railroad equipment, to noncommercial organizations in the United States may be entered, or withdrawn from warehouse, for consumption free of customs duties, fees, or charges, internal-revenue taxes, and marking or other import requirements or restrictions.*
Sect. 2. This Act shall effective as to articles entered, or withdrawn from warehouse, for consumption on or after the date of its enactment and prior to the close of December 31, 1948.
Approved June 25, 1948.

be a problem. Just weeks before the ships would sail, however, a lot of "if's" remained in the equation.

4. France in 1948

In October, Picard wrote to Pearson telling him that forty-nine boxcars were ready, and they had three Liberty ships to carry the boxcars scheduled to sail in seven weeks. It looked to Picard that the ships would make it into New York in mid-December as originally planned and well before the tax deadline that was writ into law. Whether or not all the boxcars were actually ready to go is historical guesswork because on October 18, only two of the cars were unveiled in Paris and where the others were located or the state of restoration is not known. We do know that many of the boxcars, which were first introduced in the 1870s, were in rough shape; making sure that they looked good enough cosmetically for American states to choose to keep them as monuments was one challenge; making sure that they were in good enough shape to travel across the ocean and then across the U.S. was another.

In a mid-November letter from the representative of the French National Railroads in the New York office, who signed his name only as "M. Gaveau," suggested that even if forty-nine boxcars had been selected, the job of furbishing them was far from complete. In his letter, Gaveau asks Pearson's advice on which word should be painted in bold white letters on the side of each car: "Gratitude," or "Thank You." Pearson's response to Gaveau is polite, but a tad curt: "I don't think it makes any difference exactly how the Train is painted and, therefore, I do not believe we need to bother our friends in France to change the name."

For someone who was so intimately aware of the importance of publicity, Pearson's retort was a bit disingenuous. Pearson well knew that the message does matter and so did the French. Even Cast and Picard's initial letter emphasizes the need to amplify the message of France's gratitude for America's support in war and in peace through extensive media coverage.

In addition to the work that would have to go into readying forty-nine dilapidated boxcars, the nationwide publicity campaign for individual gifts to be loaded into those boxcars had not yet begun in earnest. There had been scattered newspaper articles about the planned gift, and no doubt some people had begun knitting, crocheting, beading, sculpting, painting, drawing, or sewing something they would like to contribute, but a comprehensive publicity and collection campaign to the public had apparently not yet started.

Still, Picard doesn't seem to have been worried. The boxcars were being found and renovated and the French Gratitude Train committee members had already solicited many large gifts from institutions. In mid-October, Picard continued to express confidence that the ship would sail out of Le Havre on November 25. The letter ends by thanking Pearson for agreeing to preside over the Merci Reception and Distribution Committee in the United States, which would, he suggested, include all forty-eight governors.

Picard's assumption that there would be forty-eight U.S. governors on the committee was a little premature. Pearson's ever-present assistant, Karr, who had been so important to the Friendship Train, had begun a month earlier inviting dignitaries and members of the Friendship Train committee to participate in this project, but there was not yet what might be called a formal committee. Karr was also planning a grand reception for the Merci Train at the Waldorf Astoria in New York, even though he had doubts about the French making their own deadline. He even suspected that the ship might not arrive by the end of the year when the Joint Resolution expired. Still, plans needed to be made.

Invitations were sent, R.S.V.P.s were received. Senators, representatives, businessmen were all invited with the assurance as Pearson wrote, "There is no political flavor to the train as far as the French are concerned, and it is interesting to note that not even the Communists have opposed this gesture of friendship, apparently because it was so popular."[70] Pearson, as requested by the French, agreed to chair the committee and would handle all planning and logistics in the U.S., but he had hoped to have three honorary chairmen who would add gravitas and publicity to the effort. Pearson made a personal appeal to President Harry S. Truman, General Dwight D. Eisenhower, who had moved from the battlefield to the president's office at Columbia University, and New York Governor Thomas E. Dewey. If Truman's office responded at all,

---

[70] *Letter from Drew Pearson to Dwight D. Eisenhower. Drew Pearson papers, LBJ Library, RG 2106-7*

it was a cursory decline. General Eisenhower declined, but did so eloquently and with regret noting that, "I reach this decision very reluctantly because your letter is most persuasive and the nature of the train itself is the sort of thing that attracts me personally." [71] New York's Governor Thomas E. Dewey graciously accepted the invitation and would be seated at the gala in a place of honor at the center of the head table.

All forty-eight governors were invited to attend the festivities, and some had already accepted, but on November 22, Pearson heard from France: "Because of longshoremen's strike arrival French Thank You Train postponed until mid-January." The welcome party was put on hold.

November passed and so did most of December and no ship sailed. On December 28, 1948, Leon Pearson, Drew's brother, wrote from the National Broadcasting Company office in Paris, "Gifts for the train are still pouring in, days after the deadline, in such volume that the Committee is obliged to refuse them. The 49 cars are full to overflowing, and it's physically impossible to take anything more." [72] The year ended as did the exemption for duty and taxes that the 80th Congress had given the train. The 81st Congress convened anew on January 3, 1949, without a ship on the horizon. Encouraged by Congressman Aime Forand of Rhode Island who had served in France during World War I, Congress extended the deadline on Joint Resolution 433 in short order

---

[71] *Letter from Eisenhower to Pearson, LBJ Library, RG 2105.*
[72] *The letter from Leon to his brother is among the Drew Pearson papers in the LBJ Library. Document RG-2439, accessed by researcher Roxanne Godsey.*

and without dissent. France's "thank you" had another six months to land duty-free in America.

5. Many Thousands of Gifts

There had been some publicity about the *Gratitude Train* in French newspapers, but the nationwide campaign to collect gifts from every province was not launched in earnest until October 1948. If France's thank you was to arrive as planned on the anniversary of the *Friend Ship*'s arrival in France the year before, the "Merci" ship had to sail by the first week in December. Picard and the Merci Train committee did not give their compatriots much time to think about what exactly to send to America. This short time frame was, however, appropriate as it mirrored that of the Friendship Train, which generated a wildly successful response across the country in just four weeks.

While solicitation for donations from institutions, large donors, and dignitaries, including French President Auriol had begun much earlier, the collection from "ordinary" French people was a spontaneous response to an imminent deadline. President Auriol donated forty-nine porcelain vases from the famous French plant in Sèvres and institutions sent large works of art or historical artifacts. Many gifts were books, handcrafts, art that told a story about a family, or an experience. Though the quality of many of the hand-crafted gifts testify to months of work, many individuals gave what they had on hand or were inspired to give at the moment.

Gaston Muller was one who gave spontaneously with great heart as he found himself at the Gare d'Orsay in Paris and saw the growing mound of gifts from people like himself, piling up at the train tracks. His gift to an anonymous American was a miniature portrait framed in bronze and painted on ivory. The portrait was a blonde woman with a bow in her hair. His father had painted it and his mother had cherished it until she died, just five months after Paris was liberated. Muller's mother had been so happy to see American troops march through Paris that Gaston was compelled to put something on the train in her memory. Only later when he spoke to his sister did he realize what the token meant to her and he tried to recover it. Finding a small box carrying a three-inch ivory miniature framed in a bronze oval medallion amid so many thousands of individually wrapped gifts was, however, an impossible task.

Like Muller's, many gifts were given on the spot; others were products of a focused effort over weeks or months. There was the carefully crafted scrapbook made by the boys' school in Avranches and sent to Arizona, for example. And the forty-nine wedding dresses created and stitched by different designers in Lyon, one dress destined for each state. Hundreds of delicately stitched textiles, sculptures welded from bullet and shell casings, and dolls wearing provincial costumes were all part of the train's bounty.

Every gift was tagged with the symbol of the Merci Train – a steam engine with flowers on the pilot. The colors are the same as the French flag (blue, red, and white) and the flowers are symbolic of Flanders Field, the final resting place of many Americans who fought for France and died there in World War I.

Several translations of the gift guidelines exist, and in general they said: "The donations should not be anything necessary to rebuilding the French economy. Specifically, no food should be sent. The gifts should have a typical French character. They will call to mind France, its traditions, its charm and its culture. They will be, for example, historical, artistic, regional, folkloric artifacts. They might include glassware, crystal ware, porcelain, artistic items, leather goods, enamels, goldsmithing, bronzes, ceramics, pottery, carved wooden objects, paintings, etchings, embroidery, lace, tapestries, headdresses and provincial costumes, nativity scenes, stained glass, bells, articles of Paris, and specimens of French production and craft so famous in the world."[73]

---

[73] *Translation provided by Alexis Muller, curator of the Merci Train Facebook site.*

6. Welcome Party Redux

His colleagues in France assured Pearson that a ship bearing France's Gratitude Train would sail in mid-January for an early February arrival, and Pearson was, again, determined to put on a grand welcome. By this time Karr had offices in Washington D.C. as well as at Rockefeller Plaza in New York and he was the point person in New York. From D.C., Pearson and others in his office sent him a list of people to invite, but Karr did not appreciate all the suggestions that were coming his way. Clearly diplomacy was not his strong suit. On January 10, he penned a complaint to Pearson about his office assistant's suggestions. "Marian[74] has been sending up to me lots of people to be added to the Reception Committee for the Train. Many, if not all of the people are SOB's and genuine stinkers, not to mention stuffed shirts and hungry Wall Streeters. They are mostly Park Avenue, Fifth Avenue and a lifted pinky set. Since we have a fine reception committee shaping up, do I have your permission to ignore them?"

In the margin of the letter, Pearson scribbled a penciled "Yes."

7. The *Magellan*

In the initial planning stage, the French intended to have the Merci Train arrive in New York Harbor on December 17, one year to the day after the bounty of the Friendship Train arrived in Le Havre. Pearson received assurances that all was

---

[74] *Marian Canty was Drew Pearson's Assistant in his Washington D.C. office, 1313 – 29th Street N.W.*

going according to schedule and advised the U.S. committee chairs that the Merci Train would be loaded on December 2, on three Liberty Ships—the *Oradour*, the *Rouen*, and the *St. Lô*. The departure date proved to be optimistic, the welcome ceremonies in New York were postponed, but in the meantime, the French jettisoned the idea of three smaller ships and instead commissioned a single vessel that had the capacity to carry all forty-nine boxcars across the Atlantic.

Originally designed as a "corsair" by the Germans during the war, the *Magellan* was far larger than the Liberty ships. Built in Saint Nazaire in occupied France, the *Magellan* was 147 meters long, 18 meters wide, had a deadweight of 9325 tons, and the added advantage of spacious cabins for captain and crew. Though commissioned originally by the Germans to be used in World War II, the war ended before the ship was finished so the *Magellan* became the first French ship launched after liberation. [75] For this journey to America, in white letters ten feet high, "Merci America" was painted on the ship's black hull.

Forty-nine boxcars were lashed in the hold and the *Magellan* set sail from Le Havre at noon on Friday, January 14, 1949. Georges Huart, an employee of the French Railway (SNCF), was charged with accompanying the precious cargo. He kept a daily log and as he was a railroad man, not a seaman, his musings are full of wonder. He writes of his son, Christian

---

[75] *Information about the ship is from États-Unis - France, les élans du coeur (1947 – 1949), and from* http://uim.marine.free.fr/hisnav/archives/navires_uim/op-com/magellan-train.htm

who he dearly missed, and of the seas which became choppy as the ship powers past the lighthouse at the tip of the cape at Barfleur then churns down the channel and out to sea. Huart is far from a seasoned sailor and over the next several days, the ship's motion, which he likens to an elevator rising and falling makes him walk "as if drunk."

In his journal he describes the photo of Christian dancing with the motion of the ship across his table as he writes. The waves are relentless, the ship vibrates through the night but as the days go by, he marvels at the night sky, the immensity of space, and the seagulls ("brave little beasts!") that follow the ship well out to sea. He gives detailed accounts of the weather, which changes daily, and meals, which are delicious, and far better than what he had on shore. In France in 1949, rationing continued to limit the menu.

Georges Huart was on board because as the tension between the U.S.A. and U.S.S.R. had hardened into a Cold War, railroad executives worried, as Pearson had when the Friend Ship was docking in Le Havre, that an exchange of gifts between the people of France and the U.S could be a tempting target for communist saboteurs. To protect against that possibility, each of the boxcars was firmly lashed in place, but if any of these moorings were severed, or the "hard points" to which they were affixed loosened, the heavy cars could shift. Such a precipitous change in the ballast could cause serious damage or even cause the ship to founder. The captain recorded one frantic radio message from the port to the ship asking the ship's coordinates and news, apparently fearing they had come to some harm and all aboard sent to the bottom of the sea.[76] In fact, there were no incidents to report and the crossing was so uneventful, the captain wrote that the mid-winter crossing by the southern route along the 36th parallel was like "a Club Méditerranée cruise."[77]

Though temperatures were freezing, the day was sunny and the wind calm when, on the 1st of February 1949, Huart stood on deck watching New York rise in the west. The only problem was, the *Magellan* had arrived three days ahead of schedule and the dignitaries who were meant to be present were on the *De Grasse*, seventy-two hours away. A flurry of radio messages was exchanged as the commander of the *De Grasse* requested that the *Magellan* find a discreet anchorage to await their arrival.

With gigantic white letters clearly legible from the air announcing, "Thanks, America" painted on the black ship's hull, discretion proved impossible. Even as messages were exchanged, the *Magellan* was spotted by helicopters. As the sky darkened to night and helicopters circled above, Georges Huart was awestruck by the sight of New York City ignited with layers of multi-colored lights on buildings and cars' headlights flashing. They passed the Statue of Liberty with her crown

---

[76] *From the journal of Captain Icart,* http://uim.marine.free.fr/hisnav/archives/navires_uim/op-com/magellan-train.htm *Accessed November 26, 2018, "En intermède, au milieu du voyage un message radio très alarmé de l'Armement nous demandant position et nouvelles, le bruit ayant couru dans les milieux maritimes qu'une machine infernale avait expédié équipage et nacelle au royaume de Neptune. »*

[77] *From the journal of Captain Icart "Partis du Havre en plein hiver nous avons fait une traversée exceptionnelle de beau temps par la route du sud, le long du 36e parallèle. Si bien que notre "fier vaisseau" comme disait le Commandant, se tailla fort gentiment sa route à travers l'Atlantique."*

illuminated, her torch raised, and a pilot boat was dispatched to lead them in to a protected anchorage. Orders were exchanged in English and French and back to English, sirens sounded, lights crisscrossed the sky creating an arch of lights with the Merci Ship at the center. Two and a half hours later, at 8:30 P.M. on February 1, the *Magellan* dropped anchor at the mouth of the Hudson.

The next morning the ship was escorted by three tugs to the dock in Weehawken, New Jersey where "all that floated was decked out, everything that had a whistle or a siren greeted us with three long blows; helicopters danced a ballet and a formation of Air Force jets saluted with a fly-by...and an escort of fireboats pumped water, which fell in spears of ice on this splendid, sunny, cold winter morning."[78] It was, Huart noted, an unforgettable spectacle.

8. A Grand Welcome

The dignitaries arrived in the wake of the *Magellan* two days later on the original schedule, and though they had missed the Merci ship's arrival and escort to the dock, they did not miss the parade or the huge party at the Waldorf Astoria that Pearson and Karr had planned. On Thursday February 3, two hundred thousand people lined the streets of lower Manhattan from the Battery to City Hall. Confetti of shredded paper swirled from skyscrapers and children were released from

---

[78] *This account of the Commander of the Magellan is from the website by Christian Vilnas and accessed November 8, 2018.*
http://uim.marine.free.fr/hisnav/archives/navires_uim/op-com/magellan-train.htm

school to cheer their delight. Army, Navy, Marine and police bands played as representatives from the American Legion paraded up Broadway with New York's boxcar. At City Hall, the French Ambassador Henri Bonnet officially delivered the state's boxcar to New York's mayor, Michael O'Dwyer, and in a moving ceremony, a French war veteran raised a gold torch high for the crowd to see. Its flame had been carried from the Tomb of the Unknown Soldier in Paris. Its destination: Arlington National Cemetery.

Hundreds of people gathered at the Waldorf Astoria in New York to commemorate the arrival of the "Merci Train" boxcars, which were loaded with gifts for Americans and carried across the ocean in the hold of the Magellan. Photograph provided by the family of Charles Dhugues, a member of the French delegation of the S.N.C.F. railroad. Courtesy of Musée du Bouchardais. L'Ile Bouchard, France.

The day ended with an evening gala at the Waldorf Astoria attended by over two-hundred people dressed in stiff and shimmery formal attire. Dinner was served in the large ballroom, which was so packed with tables and chairs arranged side by side and back to back, there was hardly room for wait staff to pass. Only the dignitaries—representatives of government, unions, and business—had room to push their chair away from the table, draped in white with a single silver candlestick in the middle. The others were at round or oval tables in various sizes, with six or eight or ten places set as closely as the plates would allow. The room was full; the Merci Train and all who had accompanied it overseas had been grandly welcomed to America.

9. Ceremonies Across the Country

At least one member of the French delegation accompanied a boxcar to each capital of every state, and across the country the gesture of the Merci Train was celebrated. Crowds gathered to hear and to see the French thank you that was as unique and heartfelt as the Friendship Train had been fourteen months earlier. At the 14th Street Pennsylvania Railyards in Washington D.C. the boxcar was ceremoniously presented, speeches were made, and a private reception followed at the Carleton Hotel. To all of these events, President Truman was invited but did not attend.

The French might have understood that the president was otherwise engaged, but there was some need to explain why the president's wife refused to receive the French delegation who wanted to deliver a giant bouquet of roses personally. Robert Pyle, the American horticulturist who introduced the "Peace Rose" from Europe to America accompanied the delegation to the White House and in a letter to Pearson wrote: "To my friends in France, I have tried to explain the curious blind spot in the White House by reason of which they were unable to see the French delegates from the Thank You Train."

In Pearson's response to Pyle, he was dismissive of the Trumans, but provided no explanation. "For some strange reason the Trumans were very loath to help international good will by receiving any member of the French Gratitude Train," he wrote, "and I am not surprised that Mrs. Truman was so inhospitable in regard to the French gentlemen who had expected to accompany you to the White House with the roses."[79]

Following the events in Washington D.C., part of the delegation traveled the short three miles across the Potomac to Arlington National Cemetery. There the flame of the Tomb of France's Unknown Soldier was ceremoniously delivered to honor America's Unknown Soldier, "who rests in honored glory known but to God."[80] America's Memorial was built to honor those who died in WWII, and on that chilly day in February 1949, veterans of both World Wars were remembered; their sacrifice recalled. Then the delegation

---

[79] *Letter from Drew Pearson in the LBJ Library, Drew Pearson Archive, RG doc 1988.*
[80] *The tomb of the unknown soldier in Arlington is a white marble sarcophagus. Three Greek figures representing Peace, Victory and Valor face Washington D.C. Six wreaths sculpted on each represent the six major campaigns of WWI. Inscribed on the back are the words" Here rests in honored glory an American soldier known but to God."*

traveled the 35 miles south to Quantico for a marine tribute: a flyover, a marine guard, and the placing of a wreath at the memorial commemorating marines who died in WWI.

American Cemeteries in France honor American soldiers who died fighting for France's freedom. Many are "known but to God." Author photo May, 2018.

Flyovers were not part of the program in every capital, but there were always crowds. People gathered to hear speeches, to marvel at their state's beautifully refurbished boxcar, to listen to the stories of veterans who had fought in France, and to hear the heartfelt thanks of a member of the French delegation who expressed thanks on behalf of all French people for American sacrifices in war, and in peace. The memory of the Friendship Train was not so distant, so the scene felt familiar to many: Two trains traveling in winter, representing friendship and gratitude. The show went on for days as the gifts were unwrapped, exhibited, and ceremonially presented. Many recipients wrote personal thank you notes to the donors, completing the circle of giving and gratitude. Then each state dealt with the question: What to do with a dark gray empty boxcar adorned with colorful coats of arms?

10. Boxcar Memorials

Every state received a boxcar loaded with gifts meant to be given to Americans. Forty-four of the forty-nine boxcars have survived to honor and remember those who died in two world wars. This photo is taken by the author at the fairgrounds in Albuquerque, New Mexico.

The boxcars themselves were originally intended by Picard and Cast to be preserved as monuments to commemorate the sacrifices made by American soldiers who fought on French soil. [81] Those who had served in both WWI and WWII in France would have remembered them as crowded and dirty. Each soldier standing upright with a rifle had two

---

[81] *Locations of boxcars by state are online at mercitrain.org. The boxcars in Colorado, Connecticut, Massachusetts, Nebraska and New Jersey no longer exist.*

square feet of space.[82] They did not have seats, windows, toilets or sleeping accommodations, and made infrequent stops. To say they were uncomfortable is a significant understatement, but unless they were being transported as prisoners, these boxcars may have been remembered as relatively safe spaces. For the moment, the soldier enduring the crowded quarters of a 40 & 8 was not crouched in a waterlogged trench near Verdun in 1917, or fighting his way under heavy fire, blinded by hedgerows through a field not far from where he had landed on the beach in Normandy in 1944.

All the boxcars had been recently refurbished in France before their transatlantic voyage, freshly painted a dark gray, and decorated with brightly colored coats of arms, each unique, each representing one of France's forty provinces. The shields themselves were brilliant works of art, designed by the artist, Robert Louis, who was famous for his heraldry. On one side of the boxcar in bold white capital letters: "Train de la Reconnaissance Française," on the other side the words were translated: "Gratitude Train."

Not all forty-nine boxcars have been treated well, but forty-four have been preserved in various conditions. Briefly in 1949, the French feared that the Missouri car had been relegated to prison, but the misunderstanding was cleared up by Pearson who wrote to explain that the car had been temporarily sidelined near, and not in, a prison while it was

---

[82] *The dimensions available per soldier is from Gloria De Paola's reporting in The Merci Train Visits Woonsocket: A French Connection. Small State, Big History: The Online Review of Rhode Island History., http://smallstatebighistory.com/merci-train-visits-woonsocket-french-connection/Accessed November 3, 2018.*

awaiting its permanent home. For a while, Michigan's car was so deteriorated that a tree was growing through it, and Rhode Island's was rescued by a couple who purchased it from Crandall's junk yard in Charleston.

Many boxcars have been beautifully refurbished, though not all with attention to historical accuracy. New Mexico has two cars side by side on the fairgrounds in Albuquerque—one is the original, showing its age, which includes seventy years of exposure on the high desert; the second is a replica, a "new" old 40 & 8, which was purchased and renovated to resemble what the original car had looked like in its glory, complete with shields, when it arrived in 1949. The five cars that were sent to Colorado, Connecticut, Massachusetts, Nebraska, and New Jersey have been lost to history. Connecticut's was destroyed by fire sometime in the 1950s. Only the brass plates of Colorado's car survived and the fate of the rest of the boxcar itself remains a mystery.

In Massachusetts and New Jersey, the cars were scrapped. The saddest story is the one told by Andy Dolak about the Nebraska boxcar: "...it was shunted from place to place. It went first to the state historical society, then to the Nebraska Forty and Eight Society, and finally to a playground in the city of Lincoln. In 1951, an attempt was made to return it to the historical society, which did not want it, so it was sold to an Omaha junkyard for $45. There its wheels and metal parts were pounded into scrap and its body converted into a storage shed. Its humiliation finally ended in 1961 when the junkyard was relocated, and the box car was demolished."[83]

Nebraska's boxcar's ignominious end is redeemed by the state museum's care of many of the gifts it carried. Most of Nebraska's gifts were given away to individuals as well as public and private organizations, as the donors intended, but the Nebraska museum kept and cared for 250 pieces that otherwise might have suffered the same fate as the boxcar. Many household and personal items, toys and children's art have little inherent value, but such items are important artifacts that provide invaluable glimpses into how people lived, worked, and interpreted the stories imbedded in their surroundings. Nebraska cannot show off a boxcar, but its online exhibit is a worthy contribution to future historians of the Merci Train and its message.

11. Given in Gratitude

No one knows exactly how many gifts were sent to the U.S. in the Merci Train, though we do know that the campaign was so successful, many could not fit in the train and were left at the train station, the Gare d'Orsay. The number of gifts that made the journey across the Atlantic is most often cited as 52,000, but researchers have not yet located the ship's manifest or a detailed inventory and the surviving records from museums are inconsistent: Does a box carrying three toy cars from the same donor count as one gift or three? In any

---

[83] *From: http://mercitrain.org/Nebraska/*

event, the donations range from a unique and valuable work of art like the bust of Ben Franklin cast by the eighteenth-century neoclassical sculptor Jean-Antoine Houdon to a single postcard that was, for the donor, a special memory. Some are beautiful crafts: lacework, beadwork, carvings, miniature enamels. Others are touchstones of a moment: war medals, "trench art" which are sculptures welded and hammered from bullet and shell casings, a baby's bonnet, a doll; a tricolor strand of threads woven from a flag ostensibly flown the day Paris was liberated; a piece of an ancient bronze bell found in a cathedral's ashes; postcards of a country village that had been bombed to rubble.

Throughout the month of February 1949, at least a thousand gifts were delivered to each state capital.[84] None was auctioned, which was a restriction stipulated by the French in the later planning phases so as not to give unfair advantage to the wealthy. The gifts were meant to be given to individual Americans, but how they would be given was left to the discretion of the governor of each state. In most states, paintings and sculptures went to museums, books to libraries, toys to orphanages. It's possible, but unprovable, that politicians, committee members and volunteers who shepherded the Merci Train through their state received a token of gratitude for their efforts. Just one state, Arizona, chose to house and maintain the entire collection in the State Museum. As Arizona Governor Dan E. Garvey said at the time,

---

[84] *For many years it was believed that Hawaii received only the boxcar and none of the gifts. That theory has been disproved with extensive research by Alexis Muller.*

the only way all the people of Arizona could have the opportunity to see and appreciate the gifts was if they were kept and exhibited by the state.

In every state, the arrival of the Merci Boxcar received a grand welcome, and in some cases, with even more media coverage than the Friendship Train had received. In New York, Pearson wrote that the parade route was carefully laid out because the boxcar mounted on an army trailer weighed twenty tons, too much for some streets thinned by underground subways. In Pennsylvania, an editorial labeled the Merci Train a reciprocal response to the Friendship Train and opined that "The great value of the gifts the French have sent in return is not the intrinsic worth of the articles, but, first, the self-respecting desire of the French people to respond in kind to a friendly gesture, and second, the exchange of friendly gifts across the international barriers of oceans and boundaries, so that people speak to people, regardless of differences in their languages and distances in space." [85] Several newspapers across the country echoed that sentiment.

Many states temporarily exhibited the gifts in the capitol or state museum and then sent all or parts of the collection to towns and cities across the state. Governor Garvey's decision to keep the whole collection allowed most of Arizona's gifts to remain intact, under the protection of the state library and archives for an indefinite period. This decision gives us a clearer picture of what each boxcar might have carried. In

---

[85] *Lock Haven (PA) Express, Friday, April 1, 1949, page 4. Accessed from newspapers.com.*

other states, while the majority of gifts were disbursed, some were retained in well-preserved collections in museums and archives, some of which are now searchable on-line.[86]

Many more gifts are likely to be found, long forgotten and stored in the corner of somebody's attic, or on a little noticed shelf in a hometown library waiting to be discovered. Somewhere in America there is a small bronze miniature of a blonde woman with a bow in her hair. It was a modest gift, but great in the eyes of the donor and his sister. If you look carefully, you might see it was signed by A. Muller, the donor's father, who gave it spontaneously in memory of his mother who died not long after she celebrated American troops marching down the Champs Élysées.

---

[86] *In 1999, the late Earl R. Bennett wrote a manuscript and developed a website about the Merci Train, which continues to be maintained and is regularly updated as new discoveries are made and reported.* http://mercitrain.org/

BOOK THREE – A SAMPLING OF GIFTS

Gifts of Gratitude

The gifts that the French Train of Gratitude carried from cities and villages in France to people across America were as marvelous and as varied as the people who sent them. Children sent dolls and toys and drawings they made in school; artists sent paintings and sculptures; museums sent art; designers sent dresses and mannequins showcasing French fashion through the centuries; individuals sent books and postcards, war medals and mementos. President Auriol sent 49 Sevres vases. Boxcars were full of furniture and antiques, dishes, glassware, hand-painted crockery, and clothing typical for the area. Hundreds of knitted, crocheted, sewn items with tiny perfect stitches were neatly folded, wrapped and labeled with the name and address of the donor. In time, though, labels became separated from packages, eventually donors married, or moved, or died so now, many decades later, the origin of most of the Merci gifts can no longer be traced. In fact, most of the gifts themselves have disappeared.

On top of all those unknowns, there are other uncertainties. Records are scattered, incomplete, and in some cases, unreliable so nobody knows how many gifts were packed into the Merci Train, and nobody knows how many people donated them. Writers often say that six million donors contributed to the train, although there were somewhere in the neighborhood of 52,000 gifts. So the math doesn't add up.

But there were six million members—railroad men and veterans—of the organizations that made the Gratitude Train happen so on that level, six million is legitimate. Number of gifts? Not so sure. Researcher Alexis Muller, who curates a Merci Train Facebook page has collected and begun to analyze and map the origin of gifts from a few inventories: Arizona, Nebraska, Nevada, Oklahoma. It's enough to know that Merci Train gifts came from people from every region of France.

The Arizona collection records 572 items. If every car had about that many, there could be 28,000 or so. But some states received gifts that took up a lot of space: Indiana received a six-foot statue of *Ugolino*; Idaho has the fairly massive *Winged Victory of Samothrace*. New York squirreled away an original motor cycle somewhere; forty-nine mannequins dressed in period costumes are being quietly stored in the Metropolitan Museum of Art, and someone somewhere has a Louis XV carriage. This is all to suggest that there's a lot of sleuthing to be done.

Surely there are many gifts out there to be rediscovered and many will carry stories from the past: A moment that someone chose to share. This section is a small sampling of a dozen of those stories and it's a magpie's collection, random and without a particular design. The only constant is that at the end of 1948, someone in France put this memento on a Train of Gratitude and sent it to America.

Sagebrush Headlight: Newsletter of the Nevada State Railroad Museum, Summer 2017, 132nd edition. From the Nevada State Museum Merci Train Collection. Courtesy of the Nevada State Museum, Carson City.

1. Winged Victory of Samothrace

The original sculpture of the Winged Victory of Samothrace has a commanding presence at the top of the Grand Staircase in the Louvre. Photograph taken in the Idaho State Capitol, Boise, by John Poole.

I first encountered the story of the Merci Train on the fourth floor of Idaho's capitol rotunda in the form of a winged woman I had seen before. She was supremely elegant and utterly out of place, but quite clearly the same goddess I had seen, many years earlier, atop the grand staircase in the Louvre in Paris. She was not made of marble like the original, nor was she standing on the prow of a ship, but there was no doubt who she was: Majestic, muscled, and headless, the woman greeting me in Idaho's capitol was a plaster replica of an ancient sculpture, the *Winged Victory of Samothrace*. What in the world, I wondered, was the Goddess of Victory, also known as "Nike", doing in Idaho?

The little placard at her base told me that this plaster replica was a gift from France that had been on the Merci Train. Taking a bold step forward into the wind, she arrived in Boise with her one good wing spread wide, on February 22, 1949. The person who sent the replica of the goddess of Victory to America remains unknown, nor can we say with certainty why a replica of a 2000-year-old marble statue found in Greece in the 19th century was selected to represent France in America in the 20th, but we can guess.

She was sent because she is beautiful—even robed in plaster, this winged messenger is a breathtaking work of art. The original, sculpted of translucent white marble, was shipped to France from Greece in 1863, by the French archaeologist who found her. Though she had lost her head, she was otherwise intact and was believed to be an offering of thanks to the great gods of Samothrace after a victorious battle.

In the Louvre, she was placed at the top of the grand staircase until 1938 when the winds of war began to blow, and to protect their most valuable treasures curators removed thousands of works of art from public spaces. Nike was among the exiled, sent to the Chateaux de Valençay in central France, where she waited out the war in dark safety.

In 1947, the original sculpture emerged, as France did, from a time of darkness. In 1949, a copy of the sculpture was sent across the sea – a plaster replica of the Winged Victory, a fitting messenger sent not long after a recent victory with deep gratitude.

THE CITY OF SAINT-DIE-VOSGES-FRANCE
GODMOTHER OF AMERICA

The Arms of Saint-Dié

All that remains of THE HOUSE of AMERICA
voluntarily burned by the Germans
on November 13, 1944 - along with the greater
part of the City of Saint-Dié

COSMOGRPHIÆ

Capadociam/Pamphiliam/Lidiam/ Cilicia/ Arme nias maiorē & minorē. Colchidem/Hircaniam. Hi beriam/Albaniam præterea mltas quas fingilatim enumerare longa mora eſſet. Ita dicta ab eius nomi nis regina.

Nūc vo & hẹ partes ſunt latius luftratæ/& alia quarta pars per Americū Velputiūcvt in ſequenti bus audietur lnuenta eſt: qui non video cur quis iure vetet ab Americo inuentore ſagacis ingenij vi ro Amerigen quaſi Americi terrā / ſiue Americam dicendā: cũ & Europa & Aſia a mulieribus ſua for tita ſint nomina. Eius ſitū & gentis mores ex bis hi nis Americi nauigationibus quæ ſequunt liquide intelligi datur.

Hunc in modū terra iam quadripartita cogno: ſcēt et ſunt tres primẹ partes cōtinentes/quarta eſt inſulata: cũ omni quaqẹ mari circūdata conſpiciaſ. Et licet mare vnū ſit quẽadmodi et ipſa tellus/multis tamen ſinibus diſtinctum - & innumeris repletum inſulis varia ſibi noĩa aſſumit :queẹ in Coſmogra phiæ tabulis cōſpiciunt/& Priſcianus in tralatione Dioniſij talibus enumerat verſibus.

Circuit Oceani gurges tamen vndiqẹ vaſtus Qui quis vnus ſit plurima nomina ſumit. Finibus Heſperijs Athlanticus ille vocatur At Boreẹ qua gens furit Armiaſpa ſub armis Dicit ille piger necnō Satur.idẽ Mortuus eſt alijs:

COSMOGRAPHIÆ

How did it happen that in a small quarto published in Saint-Dié on the 25th of April 1507, under the title of "Cosmographie Introductio," the name America was proposed in the following manner?

"UP TO THIS TIME ALL THE KNOWN PARTS OF THE WORLD HAD BEEN THOROUGHLY EXPLORED. THEN AMERIC VESPUCE DISCOV-ERED A NEW CONTINENT, WHICH WILL BE DISCUSSED FORTHWITH.
I DO NOT SEE WHY THIS NEW LAND SHOULD NOT BE NAMED FOR THE MAN WHO DISCOV-ERED IT WITH SO MUCH PERSPICACITY — AMERIGE, MEANING LAND OF AMERIC, OR AMERICA. WERE NOT EUROPE AND ASIA NAMED FOR TWO WOMEN ? AS FOR THE POSITION OF THE NEW LAND AND THE CUSTOMS OF ITS INHABITANTS, THESE ARE FULLY EXPLAINED IN THE ACCOUNT OF THE FOUR VOYAGES OF AMERIC.
THE WORLD, THEN, CONSISTS OF FOUR PARTS, OF WHICH WE KNEW ONLY THE FIRST THREE, — THE THREE CONTINENTS. THE NEW FOURTH PART IS AN ISLAND — AT LEAST THAT IS THE PRESENT THOUGHT, AS THE SEA SURROUNDS IT ON ALL SIDES."

Under the sponsorship of the Duke of Lorraine, René II, the Collegium Vosagense in Saint-Dié kept in touch with the great discoveries of the Renaissance. This learned group, mainly ecclesiastical, was at the same time a focus of classical Huma-nism with Italian affinities, and an agency for printing and wood-engraving in touch with Rhenish discoveries. So it happened that a new edition of the geography of Ptolemy, planned by the Collegium, considered the new extension of the known world. Vespuce's letters, relating his travels, were also translated into Latin and discussed by Mathias Ringmann and Martin Waldseemuller in their Introduction to the Comography.

FACSIMILE AND TRANSLATION

of page 30 from the "COSMOGRAPHIÆ INTRODUCTIO" of Martin Waldseemuller, Canon of Saint-Dié, printed in 1507 on the Printing Press of Canon Gautier Lud at SAINT-DIÉ.

On this page, for the first time in history, the New World was given the name of **AMERICA**

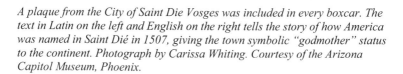

FRIENDSHIP TRAIN FROM AMERICA TO FRANCE
Winter 1947-1948
TRAIN DE LA RECONNAISSANCE FRANÇAISE AU PEUPLE AMERICAIN
Automne 1948

A plaque from the City of Saint Die Vosges was included in every boxcar. The text in Latin on the left and English on the right tells the story of how America was named in Saint Dié in 1507, giving the town symbolic "godmother" status to the continent. Photograph by Carissa Whiting. Courtesy of the Arizona Capitol Museum, Phoenix.

2. Godmother of America

In the little town of St. Dié in the northeast of France, the newly discovered continent of America was first named. The town itself has not moved, but borders have, so depending on territorial gains or losses during the most recent war at the time, St. Dié was either German or French. Today it is French, but on April 25, 1507, a German cartographer, Martin Waldseemüller printed the geographic pamphlet, *Cosmographiae Introduction* and for the first time in history named the newly discovered continent: America.

So that this story would not be forgotten, forty-nine documents, honoring that moment were printed and framed and one was nestled in every boxcar. The words in Latin and English explain that before "Americ Vespuce" discovered this new continent, the whole world was thought to be known and named. It seemed to the sixteenth-century cartographer that it was logical and correct that the name of this new "island" as it was then believed to be, should honor the man who found it. After all, Europe and Asia were both named after women so clearly it was a man's turn. That Vespucci explored only South America and not North America seems a minor detail. The main point simply made is that the City of St. Dié wanted Americans to know what had happened in their little town 500 years before and also, they wanted America to know that their town had been destroyed. In the middle of the frame flanked by the proud statements claiming the naming of America is a single photo of a shattered building, its façade crumbling and blackened. The caption reads: All that remains of "The House of America" voluntarily burned by the Germans on November 13, 1944 – along with the greater part of the City of Saint-Dié.

Several state and war museums in the U.S. have Liberty Road markers in their collections. At least two, one for Ohio, the other for Texas, arrived in the Merci Train.

3. Liberty Road Markers

After wars end, monuments are built to remember people and places. Some are grander than others, some become structures for children to climb on, and some offer a glimpse of history generations long after those who served have died. Such is the Liberty Road, which traces Patton's Third Army's advance from the beachhead in Normandy to Bastogne in Belgium. At every kilometer along the 1,146 kilometer route where soldiers marched and tanks rolled and men died, a stone marker, called a "borne", is placed.

Each borne along "La Voie de la Liberté" (Liberty Road) has a rounded top crowned with forty-eight stars representing every state from which American soldiers hailed. On the sides, the flaming torch of liberty emerging from the sea is painted just above the names of nearby towns, the dates of liberation and the division responsible. Not all of the markers that were originally cast were placed along the road; some were sent to the U.S. Some arrived for other occasions or through other routes, but at least two of these bornes found their way to the U.S. on the Merci Train.

One borne, tucked into the Texas boxcar, bears an inscription in French that translates to: *In Testimony of Gratitude*. It is fitting that Texas has such a marker as it's possible that the idea for the Liberty Road was planted in the spring of 1946, at a Texas barbeque in General Walton Walker's backyard.

Walker commanded the XX Corps of Patton's Third Army, driving relentlessly and as quickly as possible eastward through France from St. Lô to Bastogne. Under Walker's command the XXth captured Reims, crossed the Moselle River, reduced the fortress complex at Metz and broke through the Siegfried Line, earning the nickname "Ghost Corps" for the speed of its advance.[87] In March 1946, back in his home state of Texas, the Dallas Chamber of Commerce wanted to celebrate one hundred American soldiers and invited two French citizens to Dallas to bestow the honors. Guy de la Vasselais[88] had been the French tactical liaison officer to General Patton. Gabriel Hocquard was the mayor of the town of Metz, which had been liberated by Walker and the XX Corps. Both men who had known General Walker in battle were invited to Dallas and stayed at Walker's ranch for a month as the general's honored guests.

It is easy to imagine that during their stay, these three men, who each had a role in France's liberation, talked about how to commemorate those who had fought their way eastward from Normandy to Belgium. It is not such a stretch to think that Walker, Hocquard, and Vasselais began to imagine that the best way to remember such a campaign is not with a single monument planted in the ground, but with one that moves—a ribbon of highway from Normandy to Belgium. We don't know if the two French men made a specific plan as they traveled back to France. What we do know is that shortly after their return from America, Hocquard and Vasselais formed a committee, commissioned an artist, and received permission from agencies to mark the road. "La Voie de la Liberté" officially opened on September 17, 1947.

Guy de la Vasselais was elected mayor of St. Symphorien, and later became a senator in the French government. He was

---

[87] *The description of Walker's advance is from the Encyclopedia Britannica.*
[88] *Guy De La Vasselais would also play a key role in the Merci Train collection and distribution.*

among the honored French contingent on the Merci Train and accompanied the French gifts to the Western states where he had been a guest of General Walker. On that trip, he had honored the veterans of Texas, and received tributes in return.

Ohio also received a borne. It arrived on February 10, 1949 and is perfectly preserved in the state museum's archives in Columbus. The Ohio marker is inscribed with the names: Saint Servans on the Sea, and Ile-et Vilaine, which is seventy miles inland. It's a stretch of road where the 83rd Division fought from August 6 – 17, 1944. Exactly why the borne was included among Ohio's gifts is not clear, but here's a guess.

The shoulder patch of the 83rd Division was designed during World War I when the 83rd was a draftee division, most of the draftees were from Ohio, and they all trained at Camp Sherman. For this exclusively Ohio outfit, an insignia was designed with a black triangle pointed downward, inside of which is a gold circle monogrammed with the letters O-H-I-O.

By WWII, the war commemorated by the Liberty Road, the division was no longer an Ohio unit, but the shoulder patch continued to identify the men of the 83rd. Maybe that's why the borne from these two towns not far from Normandy was added to the car bound for the Buckeye State and

The shoulder patch of the 83rd Division graphically spells the name of the state where the draftees were from in WWI: Ohio

maybe it was destined to go to any state, representing every state that had given so many young lives in two wars.

154

After the bombing, not much survived of Mme. Bouthier's home, but she sent a slightly chipped treasure on the Merci Train. In her note, she apologized that the dish was not perfect. Photograph by Mary W. Covington. Courtesy Nevada State Museum, Carson City.

4. Limoges Candy Dish

On June 15, 1944, a formation of American Flying Fortresses bombed Angouleme, France. Their target was the German-held railway station, which they mostly missed, destroying instead over four hundred homes and killing nearly 300 civilians. Mme. Bouthier did not die, but everything she

155

owned was shattered, lost, broken, burned. Almost everything. Mme. Bouthier was not broken. She had lived; many had not. And it was, after all, not the Germans, but the Americans who had bombed her city. Her enemies were not in the air that day; her enemies were the Nazis who had occupied her village four years earlier. Dozens of her neighbors had been shot for resisting; nearly four hundred had been deported to Auschwitz. Eight would return.

After years of war, Mme. Bouthier and her neighbors were accustomed to hardship. The guns had stopped in 1945, but the summer of 1946 brought drought, crops failed, and the winter of 1946-47 was brutal. There wasn't enough coal or wood for warmth; there wasn't enough food. Their region was devastated, but they could and did help themselves. They made vases and tiny toys from metal casings and dolls from scraps of material. They raised rabbits and chickens to supplement rations and in 1947, the birth rate exceeded the death rate for the first time since 1940.

The years of war had been tough, but Mme. Bouthier was neither broken nor bitter; she was grateful to America. She was grateful to the American boys who paid for her freedom with their blood. To accompany her gift of a candy dish, with small upright letters she penned a short note: "If my means and my gratitude were equal, you would be receiving a truly beautiful souvenir from my country. But I'm 64 years old and at present, the old are very poor in France, especially if they are disaster victims who lost everything, as I am. As a disaster victim, I've been the grateful recipient of aid from our American friends and cannot let the Merci Train depart without giving a very modest object, which bears the very evidence that it lived through the bombings of June 19, 1944. With all my heart and friendship, I thank you."

Mme Bouthier knew that her home and all that was in it had been destroyed by the Allies as they attempted to dislodge the German occupiers, but many had lost much more than she. In the end, the Americans, to whom her small, chipped candy dish would go, had given her and France something more precious: freedom.

5. Watercolor of James R. McConnell's gravesite

James R. McConnell, American pilot, one of the first to fly for France in World War I. Photo courtesy of the Mayor of Flavy-le-Martel, provided to the author in May 2018.

In 1915, James Rogers McConnell left the University of Virginia to become one of the first seven Americans to volunteer to fly for France in World War I. A year later, this band of American pilots under French command would become known as the "Lafayette Escadrille." On March 19, 1917, McConnell was killed in a dogfight in eastern France and though he never returned to the university campus, he would be remembered.

On the plaza near Clemons Library, a bronze male angel called *The Aviator* is perched with its massive wings outstretched, one muscled leg stepping forward into the wind. Created by Gutzon Borglum, who is better known for his outsized sculpture of four presidents on Mount Rushmore, the twelve-foot high angel with an eight-foot wingspan was funded by McConnell's classmates who "remembered his ambition, courage, and pursuit of excellence in all endeavors."[89] Their memorial is not the only work of art honoring McConnell. A watercolor of his gravesite in the field in France where he fell was sent on the Merci Train to the United States.

---

[89] *From an article in UVA Today* https://news.virginia.edu/content/uva-honors-inspiration-winged-aviator-statue-100-years-after-his-death

An original watercolor in vibrant colors of James R. McConnell's gravesite near Flavy-le-Martel in France arrived as a gift from the artist on the Merci Train. Painted by the young artist, Lucien Cahen-Michel. Photo by Mary W. Covington. Courtesy of the Nevada State Museum, Carson City.

The artist, Lucien Cahen-Michel, was nearly the same age as the young American pilot when he was shot down. Cahen-Michel would live to become a well-known painter, but one day in October, seven months after McConnell fell not far from Flavy-le-Martel, he simply painted what he saw: A simple memorial for McConnell, who died five days after his thirtieth birthday. Above the wooden cross bearing his name feathered flags point to a mottled violet sky. The flags, gently unfurling in the breeze look like the headdress of the Lakota Sioux, the symbol for the Lafayette Escadrille.

Later, McConnell's remains were moved to the Lafayette Escadrille Memorial near Paris, where his name is etched in stone. Three decades would pass, and another war would be fought, but in 1949, thirty-two years after McConnell's death, Lucien Cahen-Michel gave his painting to America. Now perfectly preserved in the Nevada State Museum, the watercolor is vibrant, a tribute to a life, which McConnell himself chronicled. His autobiography, *Flying for France,* could not, however, have included how, decades later, he would be remembered and how one artist would choose to thank him for his service with a gift to America.

6. A Letter to Friends

The first page of Madame Dupont's long letter about living in occupied France during World War II. Courtesy of Nevada State Museum, Carson City.

On 25 November 1948, a woman named Madame Robert Dupont from a little village of Montabon, with a "population of 600 and a XII-century church," wrote a long letter that begins "Dear American Friends." She introduces her husband, Robert, who was an artist and his brother, Gabriel, who was a musician. They both achieved some level of fame, but her gift is neither her husband's art nor her brother-in-law's music. She included with her letter a "book about France, our country old and dear" and postcards that showed how cellars in the region were built into the rock, which was light and porous.

But Madame Dupont's real gift was her letter, which is about living in Montabon during the war, an area that was occupied and frequently bombed. It is a snapshot of resistance, leavened with dry humor and a touch of sarcasm. By her count, her home was bombed thirty-six times because she lived close to the tracks used by the German trains. One can imagine this woman, scratching tick marks in the wall after each attack, noting the damage, nodding in appreciation that she and the house had survived. We can't really know what she did, but we can imagine what we might do after the first bombing, then the second, then the fifteenth...the thirtieth.

We can know that the region was devastated by enemies but also by friends. As Madame Dupont wrote in her letter: "Our military planes knew about this location, so they did a great job bombing those tracks! What a joy when they bombed the bridge! Everything shook; our house started dancing but luckily our walls got only cracked and the ceiling got damaged just a little bit."

163

Madame Dupont and Robert stayed on, their health was not great, and in any event, there was no place to go. Germans were everywhere including those cellars carved out of that porous rock on the hillside featured in the postcards she sent. The caves were good for wine cellars; also good for the Germans who, she wrote, "transformed them into comfortable offices. They probably intended to stay for a long time." They no doubt intended to stay for the duration of the Third Reich, which was supposed to be a thousand years, a goal the Allies obliterated. They did stay four years and two months, which is a long time to share space with occupiers armed to kill, but Mme Dupont does not dwell on that detail. She does note that, "Part of the movie *La Bataille du Rail* was filmed in our region," implying, active resistance, maybe even sabotage, which is what the movie is about.

In some of the cavernous rooms in the hillside, the Germans stored "huge tanks with a corrosive liquid." She wrote that as Patton and Leclerc advanced towards the town, the Germans dumped this liquid into the reservoir, which was piped to the Loir, a small river that is not the big river (the Loire) but runs parallel to it. "All the fish died, and the smell spread through the countryside. What a joy to watch the Germans running away, putting their luggage on wheelbarrows and toy cars! All the country was crying its happiness and cheering on your nice soldiers and your military vehicles."

She ends with an apology for the long letter, "but whenever I write to my friends I get carried away." And then, as an afterthought a final postscript: "Don't give the Rhine to the Germans, it would be a big mistake."

Four pen and ink drawings, each rich with symbolism, were sent on the train by R. and M. Lesieur. Photograph by Mary W. Covington. Courtesy Nevada State Museum, Carson City.

7. A Prussian Toad

The donor and the artists remain a mystery, but the symbolism that permeates each of their four drawings, dated between 1914 and 1915, has not been diminished by time or distance. The renderings, carefully sheathed for their trip across the ocean are well-preserved, measure just over 19 inches tall and 13 inches wide and were created by two artists who shared a surname, but not an inkwell. "R" Lesieur used black ink; "M" Lesieur drew in brown. Were they husband and wife? Father and son? We don't know how or even if they were related, but we can appreciate what they left us to ponder.

There are several discrete subjects in each work, but they are linked to one another to tell a short story about a long history. Each shows a dominant and identifiable geographic feature, snippets of French culture, history, architecture and French heroes during times of war: Napoleon, Jeanne d'Arc, and Georges Clemenceau. During the Great War when they were drawn and dated, these images were printed hundreds of times on postcards to encourage resistance during the war as they simultaneously celebrate an ancient past and caution against an enemy that threatens the future.

In one of the drawings, most of the page is filled with the square in front of the Town Hall in Noyon, sixty miles north of Paris. Its iconic fifteenth-century Fountain of Dauphin in the center is easily recognizable. To the left of the fountain and nearly matching its pointed shape is a cleric, whose beard and miter identify him as Saint Médard, the fifth-century bishop of the cathedral. The bishop is standing on the left side of the frame with his right hand raised in blessing; his left hand is pouring water on the ground, perhaps, as one scholar suggested, symbolizing rain. But it also may well be the water of baptism spilling from his urn as St. Médard symbolically washed the earth at the cathedral in Noyon where Charlemagne was crowned King of the Franks in 768.

Charlemagne did much to unite the Roman Empire and to ignite a light of learning in an age where illiteracy was the norm. Crowned Holy Roman Emperor in 800, he populated his court with intellectuals and ushered in the Carolingian Renaissance, a period during which schools flourished, art and literature were celebrated, books were written. Women read. This explains the two women wearing medieval dress and reading books by candlelight etched above the cathedral in the upper left corner of the print.

At the bottom of the page, crawling on webbed hands towards the viewer is a fat soldier wearing a spiked helmet branded with an eagle. He is shaped like a toad and though his visage occupies little space, the image of his lumpen body crawling on webbed hands beneath Noyon's deserted town square is disturbing. Save the bishop and the two reading women, there is only one witness to this amphibious Prussian with his helmet-hooded eyes and braided epaulets. Just behind him peeking out from beneath the cathedral is a head of a lamb, in Christian iconography, a symbol for Jesus.

The war to end all wars finally ended four years after the Germans had occupied Noyon. By August 1918, eighty percent of the town was destroyed, and the original fifteenth-century Fountain of Dauphin was rubble. But this and three other drawings, each with many layers of stories to tell, survived to be sent in gratitude on the train to America.

Though the cars were different colors, styles, models and sizes, every boxcar included a set of Renault toy cars. Photograph by Carissa Whiting. Courtesy of the Arizona Capitol Museum Merci Train Collection.

8. Renault Toy Cars

Renault toy cars in green, red, blue, and bright yellow, were included in every boxcar. Wisconsin's inventory of gifts lists the donor simply as "the manufacturers" and it's a pretty good guess that the person who authorized sending hundreds of toy cars overseas understood that what the French automobile manufacturer needed after the war was a big car market and an image makeover. They needed a new image and brand recognition that did not associate them with the collaborationist Vichy government and distinguished them from another lightweight vehicle then in production in Europe: Germany's Volkswagen.

The Renault story is a messy one because Louis Renault's company, located in occupied France, manufactured thousands of vehicles for the German army, and for that he paid with his life after the war. The bare facts are that in 1939, Louis Renault traveled to America to request tanks to help France in the war against Germany. By the time he returned to France in 1940, his country had surrendered, the Franco-German Armistice had been signed and France was divided into the occupied territory that included Paris and environs, and a theoretically "sovereign" France in the southeast with a capital in Vichy. Under a series of leaders, Vichy France was unquestionably in Germany's pocket (which is why French soldiers fired on the Allies landing in North Africa, but that's another story).

Predictably, with France subdued in 1940, Germany wanted to commandeer the Renault factory for their own uses. To that end, executives from the German car maker Daimler-Benz and military personnel visited the Renault factory in Billancourt and began planning the factory's relocation along with its entire French workforce. Both machines and manpower would be absorbed by Daimler-Benz and moved to Germany. Renault, who had been awarded the Legion of Honor in World War I, successfully resisted the move by making an agreement with Germany: He agreed that his factory would make vehicles for the Wehrmacht in France. By doing so he later argued that he preserved 40,000 French jobs and the manufacturing plant. After the war was over, he also suggested that some of the vehicles destined for Germany were sabotaged so they would fail in the field. While keeping the factory certainly allowed jobs to stay in France and no doubt some of the 30,000 vehicles that went to Germany suffered mechanical problems, critics alleged that his claims to clandestine resistance were unconvincing. He was, they insisted, a collaborationist and profiteer and he needed to pay for his crime.

When France was liberated, Louis Renault was arrested, but he was never charged and never went to trial. Before he had his day in court he was beaten by unknown assailants while in custody and died in jail. Renault's death was high-profile, but it was far from an isolated case as politicians, vigilantes, former soldiers, and ordinary citizens of France navigated the difficult territory of becoming again one country.

In 1945, a few months after Renault's death, De Gaulle nationalized the company, retaining the name, but without compensation to his heirs, an event that would generate a lawsuit[90] many decades later. The immediate problem facing the managers of the newly state-owned car company was that they needed to sell cars and to do so, they needed foreign markets. Leadership was in place: Pierre Lefaucheux was an accomplished industrialist, a national WWI hero, and a distinguished leader of the Resistance. Fortuitously, too, Renault engineers had secretly been working on an innovative car design for the post-war economy: a rear-engine design named the 4CV, which was light, inexpensive, and a significant departure from the upscale brand that the company was accustomed to producing.

Convinced that these less expensive cars were the way to go, Renault began manufacturing and marketing these new cars and, likely as part of a promotional campaign for potential U.S. customers, models the size of children's hands found their way into every boxcar of the Merci Train. They are toys, but

---

[90] *In 2011, seven of Louis Renault's grandchildren took the state to court, arguing that nationalizing the firm was a "violation of fundamental legal and property rights." According to the BBC, the case sparked outrage in France as Communists and Holocaust survivors accused the family of trying to rewrite history. In 2012, the case was decided; the heirs lost.*
https://www.bbc.com/news/world-europe-16512081

they are also an example of French ingenuity, craftsmanship, and resilience. The 4CV became the first French car to sell over a million units.

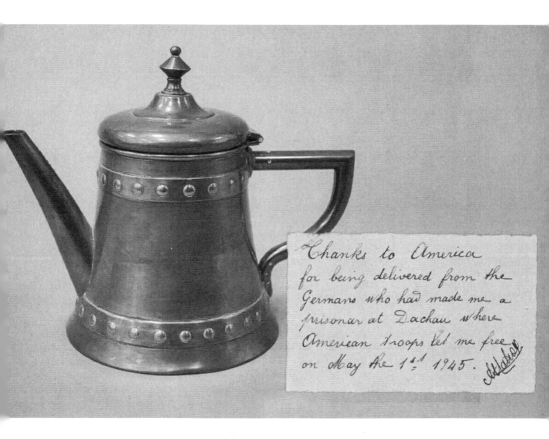

Thanks to America for being delivered from the Germans who had made me a prisoner at Dachau where American troops let me free on May the 1st 1945.

A copper teakettle from a prisoner at Dachau who wanted to thank America for his liberation. Photograph by Mary W. Covington. Courtesy Nevada State Museum, Carson City.

9. A Copper Tea Kettle from Dachau

On April 29, 1945, American troops liberated the Nazi Concentration Camp at Dachau. Two years later, a former prisoner sent his thanks on the Merci Train in the form of a copper teakettle six and a half inches tall. Enclosed in the package was his business card: Alfred Nahon, Plumber, 13 Place de la Bouquerie, Nimes. On the back of the card, which is rose pink, he wrote in brown ink in perfectly rounded script:

173

"Thanks to America for being delivered from the Germans who had made me a prisoner at Dachau where American troops let me free on May the 1st, 1945."

The teakettle itself is made of copper burnished to a smooth finish and belted twice with rings of brass that look as if they're buttoned in place with rivets. The handle, too, is brass and emerges in a strong straight horizontal line from the upper belt, but the angle softens like an arm and a hand placed delicately on the hip of the lower belt. The kettle is crowned with a rounded diamond of brass set on a bell-like pedestal and topped with a small brass ball. It's finely made.

We don't know when Monsieur Nahon was arrested or for how long he was imprisoned in Dachau. Initially built just as Hitler came to power in 1933 to re-educate Communists and Socialists, Dachau's role expanded to include those who were Jewish, homosexual, handicapped, guilty of crimes or simply of thinking independently. We cannot know much about the sender, but seventy years after Alfred Nahon, plumber, sent his gift of thanks to the train going to America, we can know that concentration camps like Dachau existed because ordinary people looked away.

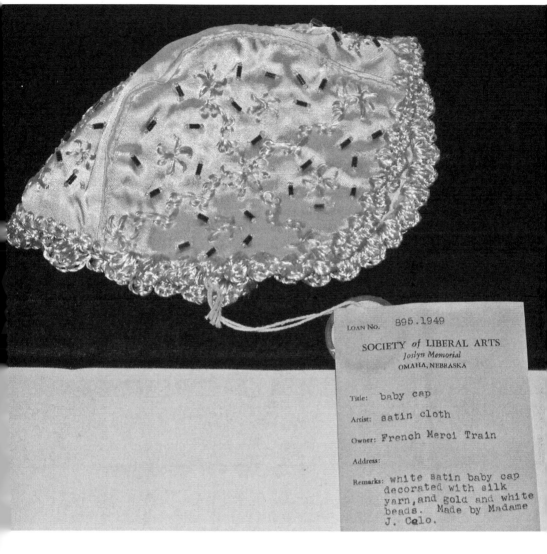

Nebraska's collection includes examples of beadwork and embroidery like this baby cap, which can be viewed, along with many other Merci artifacts, on the museum's website. Photograph from History Nebraska, 7144-166.

10. The Statue of Liberty and a Beaded Bonnet

As Drew Pearson traveled with the Merci Train across the nation, he frequently repeated that the Merci Train was the second time America had received such a gift. The first gift was the Statue of Liberty, sent from the French to commemorate the centennial of the end of America's Revolutionary War. Auguste Bartholdi was the French sculptor who designed the statue that would symbolize freedom and democracy, Gustave Eiffel (who built the Eiffel Tower in Paris) built the iron framework beneath the copper plating. Lots of fundraising efforts were conducted on both sides of the Atlantic, and work on the colossal woman went on for nine years round the clock. After every detail was complete from her eight-foot face to her twenty-five-foot feet, she was dismembered, packaged securely in 214 crates and sailed across the ocean. The passage was not a smooth one, but *Liberty Enlightening the World* made it safely into New York Harbor on June 17, 1885. The name of the French ship carrying this iconic gift was *Isère*, and the name of one young crew member was J. Calo. He was nineteen years old.

Sixty-two years later, J. Calo's wife delicately embroidered a satin baby cap with a finely stitched vine made of silk yarn, around which small rectangular gold and white beads flit like fireflies. The cap sailed to America on the Merci Train in a boxcar bound for Omaha, Nebraska, and it was accompanied by a note that she, Madame Calo of 58 Avenue Victor-Hugo in Morbihan, had made the bonnet herself and she would like to know the name of the American baby who got it. Then she delicately stitched a story, linking the tiny cap with the colossal statue delivered to New York Harbor on the *Isère* on which her husband had sailed. The cap was never given to an American baby, but it has been well preserved by the Nebraska State Museum. Its stitching still perfect, the satin still white and the tiny flowers seem to shine.

11. Triumphant Flags

An American flag, sewn by hand, to celebrate liberation day. Photograph from the Marjorie Russell Clothing and Textile Research Center by Mary W. Covington. Courtesy of the Nevada State Museum, Carson City.

It was against the laws of the Reich to fly any foreign flags in occupied France so between France's surrender to the Nazis in 1940 and its liberation in 1944, the only flags that flew in occupied France were the German national flag or the swastika of the Nazi party. All that changed when the Allies landed on the beaches of Normandy and with the help of the Resistance began the liberation of towns across the country. For four years, any display of disloyalty to the Reich—listening to foreign broadcasts, reading foreign press, flying flags or symbols other than those of Germany—were all crimes punishable by imprisonment or death. Neighbors spied and informed on each other. When Allied leaflets spilled from the sky, they were surreptitiously pocketed to be read in privacy. One could not risk reading such propaganda in public.

Despite the danger, well before liberation a donor named Madame René Vedy bought red, white and blue material to make an American flag. She carefully cut forty-eight five-pointed stars from the white fabric and stitched them by hand to the cobalt blue corner. The red was vibrant, the white unstained, and the blue the deepest she could find. In her note, she wrote that she made the flag "under the eyes of the Germans" so she would be ready to salute the Americans when they came through.

Lise Grillot, whose father was a policeman in Montcerf also wanted to be ready to welcome the liberating armies and fashioned a dress mimicking the red, white and blue stripes of the French flag. One pocket is an American flag; the other a British ensign which was at that time also the flag of Canada.

There were many such tributes to America and to liberated France as wave after wave of Allies swept east, pushing the Germans across the border through Belgium back to Germany. In their wake, French and American flags fluttered from balconies and windows. A particularly important memento was fashioned from two flags that were, so the story goes, flying from the top of the Eiffel Tower on Liberation Day. Both flags are red, white, and blue, one French, the other American. Merci Train records suggest that these two Liberation Day flags were made into a streamer of twined threads, "kilometers long," then cut and put as a souvenir into each of the boxcars as a gift from the Paris Committee and E.L. Blanchet.

This "Liberation Dress" belonged to Lise Grillot from Montcerf. The picture on the bodice is of Charles DeGaulle, symbol of resistance. Pictured here without the plain white belt and with permission of John Irving and the Benton County Historical Society in Oregon.

Whether or not these strands of thread were ever actually parts of American and French flags flown from the top of the Eiffel Tower on Liberation Day has not been proved, but authentic or not, the symbolism is meaningful: Threads of two red, white, and blue flags representing two sovereign nations, were twisted to make a single strand, unified in purpose. Eight months after Paris was liberated, General Dwight D. Eisenhower accepted Germany's unconditional surrender in a corner room on the second floor of a school in Reims.

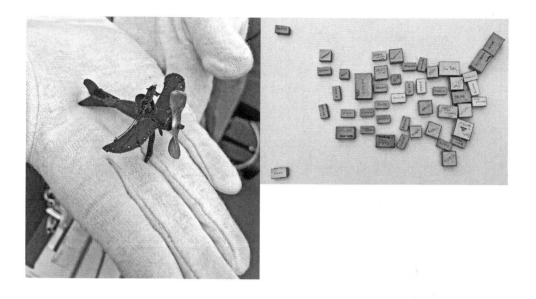

From the From the detritus of war, soldiers and artisans fashioned many things: vases, lighters, letter openers. Tiny trinkets like this airplane fashioned carefully from metal scraps were all boxed and labeled – one for each state. Every toy is smaller than a child's hand and each was packaged in a custom-made "match box.". The entire collection, missing a few states, is in Arizona's archive. Photograph courtesy of the Arizona Capitol Museum, Merci Train Collection.

12. Trench Art

During WWI, a category of art labeled "trench art" evolved as the detritus of war was used to make something functional, like smoking or writing equipment, or something beautiful like rings, photo frames or miniatures. Several of these artifacts were sent to America on the Merci Train and many are elegant testimony to the human capacity to derive beauty from misery or meaning from despair.

On the Belgian front, where an estimated 60 million shells were blasted between the French and the German trenches, elegant rings emerged, fashioned from the aluminum fuses and washers removed from incoming German shells. These were melted down, poured into molds, then filed, engraved and polished. Cartridges were shaped into crucifixes with a Christ figure welded from a melted bullet. Shell casings were elaborately decorated, often in floral motifs and often personalized. The Arizona Merci collection includes tiny metal toys that may have been fashioned from shrapnel and twisted bits of wire. Each miniature is neatly boxed and labeled with a state's name.[91]

Despite the adjective "trench" to describe the origin of the art, most of it was not created in the trenches, but behind the lines by off-duty soldiers, blacksmiths, or Royal engineers to alleviate boredom. Soldiers far from the line of fire could lose themselves making something to send home to be cherished, or to be sold to supplement meager wages. Some of the work that arrived in Merci boxcars came with notes like the one that accompanied a vase hammered from an artillery shell: "Part of the little things we found in the ruins of our house that was stricken in 1940, was this vase, a piece of memories from the 1914 war. A former soldier is sending it to you. Thanks again." That's all he wrote. Perhaps part of the note has been lost; perhaps the word "again" is a reference to America entering on the side of the French twice: the first time in 1917, the second in 1942.

---

[91] *Originally there were no doubt 49 tiny toys, but a few have been lost.*

An example of more ornate trench art: a vase hammered from a shell casing.
Photograph by Mary W. Covington. Courtesy of Nevada State Museum,
Carson City.

Sometimes an artifact is adorned with specific names, initials, battles, or a note from the sender. Idaho, for example, received a letter opener, its handle belted in tiny bronze rings and topped with a single fleur-de-lis. It's made from an artillery shell and was meant to be given to an American soldier living in North Carolina, who fought in France in 1918. Perhaps the sender fought side by side with a North Carolinian whose name he had forgotten or never knew. Survival, I think, sometimes requires a certain anonymity. With twisted wire, the sender tacked a card to the gift that it was made by a French soldier in Verdun in 1916.

Many Merci Train collections and every military museum contain examples of trench art, a rich vein of study for scholars. The range of what was created is large and each piece provides a glimpse of how one soldier chose to remember the war by carefully carving names or dates or names of battlefields. Other objects with intricately molded floral motifs or religious figures might have allowed the artist to leave the trenches for a moment as he focused on a memory or a hope.

The trench art that arrived in America on the Merci Train has not been studied and it's possible that some of it is an example of twentieth-century Chinese entrepreneurship. In Nicholas Saunders' engaging book about the subject, [92] he writes that during WWI, there was a Chinese labor corps in France that found out what regiments were in the area, acquired their badges, then made and sold souvenirs to the

---

[92] Nicholas J. Saunders book Trench Art: Materialities and Memories of War (2011), an engaging study of trench art.

soldiers, many on speculation. Some were made to order with the soldier's name.

The soldiers who crafted art from the detritus of war will for the most part remain unknown, but the art itself provides a glimpse into WWI's Western Front where men attacked and counter-attacked along a meandering line of fortified trenches that snaked from the North Sea to Switzerland. The line moved little from 1914-1918, but for all its horror, the war also left many stories that recall man's humanity to man. One is of the Christmas Truce in 1914[93], when soldiers from both sides serenaded one another with Christmas carols in their respective languages, sometimes emerging from their muddy trenches to mingle in "No Man's Land" where bodies of colleagues had recently fallen. Many other stories are found in the treasury of art that so many soldiers created to transform misery into a memory worth keeping. Some of those came to America, with gratitude.

---

[93] *Christmas Truce of 1914, https://www.history.com/topics/world-war-i/christmas-truce-of-1914, published by the A&E Television Networks, Accessed November 1, 2018.*

Every boxcar included a wedding gown created by fashion centers in Lyon, France. Some, like this one in the Marjorie Russell Clothing and Textile Research Center, have never been worn. Photo by Mary W. Covington. Courtesy of Nevada State Museum, Carson City.

13. Wedding Gowns from Lyon

France has always been known for its "haute couture," and after the war was a good time to remind Americans that France was still a fashion leader. Perhaps partly to advertise their considerable skill to an American clientele, but also as a generous gift to one lucky bride in each state, designers in Lyon created forty-nine unique wedding dresses, some of which have been preserved in state museums.[94]

Such high fashion requires a customer to measure and pamper and fit, but there were no pre-selected brides to wear the Merci Train wedding dresses and the French gave no direction about who should receive a dress so state governors could decide. Some of the dresses have never been worn but were retained in splendor in museum collections. Records of many are scanty, but a few of the dresses were given very publicly to young women who applied to be the lucky "Bride to Be."

Some states had contests, others simply an application process. In Alabama, the sole requirement was that the bride fit the dress, which was somewhere between a size 14 and 9, or comparable to a 0-2 in today's sizing. The sub-head in a newspaper article announcing the winner noted: "Clara Anne Day Chosen Because Slight Figure Suitable to No. 9 Dress." The article goes on to note that after publication of the opportunity to borrow the dress for their weddings, several women showed up at the World War Memorial Building, but "very few applicants were of the right size."[95]

---

[94] *Other dresses besides the ones noted have local stories. Miss Esther Dupre Gregorie of South Carolina was married in the dress made by Lyon designers, Mesdames Charvet and Ladous . The South Carolina dress was satin brocaded in leaf design with plunging neckline, fitted midriff, long sleeves, and a draped bustle back and long train.*
[95] *Newspaper clippings about the Alabama wedding gown and bride were made available to the author by M. Guy Jouteux from the Merci Train exhibit at the Musée du Bouchardais not far from Paris, May 2018. Unfortunately, the name of the newspaper is unknown.*

In Illinois, the requirement was that the bride had to fit the dress and the groom had to have been a WWII veteran who fought in France. Miss Millicent Hill of Winnetka, Illinois, was evidently a little late in the application process as she received a note from the State Historical Library in May, thanking her for her interest, but letting her know that applications were already under review. Fortunately for her and for inexplicable reasons despite its tardiness, Miss Millicent's application moved into the "to be considered" pile, which included about a dozen qualified applicants. In his congratulatory letter, Illinois Governor Adlai Z. Stevenson wrote, "...it is most appropriate that the dress go to the first June bride of a veteran of World War II, who served in France."[96] It's possible that Millicent's win was a result of a fortuitous choice of the earliest June date, but it's also possible that her groom's war record may have tipped the balance in her favor. Theodore Dudley was an infantry sergeant who fought in France, Belgium, and Germany. Cited for exemplary conduct in ground combat Sergeant Dudley earned a bronze star. In June 1949, wearing a designer gown from France, Miss Millicent became Mrs. Theodore Dudley.

In Connecticut, one hundred and fifty applicants were narrowed to six, all of whom met the basic requirements: a 24-inch waistline and a wedding planned for June. Neither the winner, Miss Connie Eaccarino of New Haven, nor any of the other contestants were aware that Connecticut donors had

---

[96] *Pictures and letters to Miss Millicent Hill are available on the mercitrain.org website on the Illinois tab.*

banded together to enhance the prize. In addition to the dress, "Miss Eaccarino and her fiancé, John H. Farrell III, would also receive a set of sterling silver, a wedding band, a wedding cake, a going away hat, a new suit and shoes for John, and best of all, a honeymoon trip to Europe where they would meet the women who had made her gown. The other five finalists also were given prizes, including a week at Schroon Lake Resort for the first runner up and her groom."[97] Not to be outdone, in Alabama the Montgomery Chamber of Commerce and the Zonta Club gave their chosen newlyweds, Mr. and Mrs. Myron Turner, a "bridal shower" which included passage to France for their honeymoon.

---

[97] *The reporting about the Connecticut dress is by Roxanne Godsey, Merci Train researcher, and Celia Roberts, librarian in Canton, CT. This report and letters were accessed on the Merci Train website, November 1, 2018.*

14. Ugolino and His Sons

The replica of Jean-Baptiste Carpeaux's Ugolino and His Sons was sent to Indiana on the Merci Train and was given to the University of Indiana at Bloomington where it remains today near the entrance to the Indiana Memorial Union. Photograph courtesy of Indiana University Archives.[98]

The original sculpture crafted by Jean-Baptiste Carpeaux in the middle of the nineteenth century is just over six and a

---

[98] *Photo Ugolino and his Sons" by Jean-Baptiste Carpeaux is from the Indiana University Archives Photograph Collection, Image P002135; Accession 200/3 Identified in the photo (L to R) Professor Robert Laurent, Chair of the Fine Arts Department Henry Radford Hope, and IU Director of Communications Lawrence Wheeler.*

half feet tall, nearly five feet around and weighs five thousand pounds. The plaster replica that made its way to Indiana in the Merci Train is about the same size, but it is made of plaster and considerably lighter. *Ugolino and His Sons,* is based on the story told by Dante Alighieri in the thirty-third canto of his fourteenth-century epic poem, *Divine Comedy.* The story is that of Count Ugolino from Pisa and his sons and grandsons as they died of starvation in the first, the "Inferno" section of the poem.

Ugolino is at the center of the sculpture, every muscle taut, his toes and hands clenched. The fingers of his left hand are hooked on his lower lip. One son is seated on the ground, grasping his father's muscled legs, the other is standing, leaning into his father's waist, head bowed. One grandson is fading, supported by the bodies of his father and grandfather. The other child may already be dead, his small body is slumped under his father, his head has fallen forward on his chest, his right hand slack.

It's a disturbing image, as is the Canto on which it is based. It describes a part of Dante's journey in the ninth circle of hell, where Ugolino is chained, continually chewing on the head of Archbishop Ruggieri, who imprisoned them. As his fate in hell is to starve to death with all of his descendents, the Count begins to eat his own fingers, but it upsets his children, so he stops, and the children die one by one. In a chilling passage, Dante writes: "Famine did what sorrow could not do."

The replica of this thoughtful yet disturbing work, sent in gratitude to America is placed in Bloomington, at the entrance to the Indiana Memorial Union on the university campus. No documentation survives to identify the French donor, but documentation is not really necessary. Carpeaux's sculpture simply invites the viewer to imagine and to mourn man's inhumanity to man, and to think, perhaps, about the world one is complicit in creating through action or silence.

Students throughout France painted and drew pictures to send on the Merci Train. Photograph from History Nebraska, 7144-53.

15. Children's Drawings

Their work, which arrived in Nebraska's boxcar, is clearly the product of a delightful class project at Ecole de la Trinité, 16 rue de Milan in Paris. The teacher is not named, but the assignment included drawing the outlines of the continents of North America and Europe, which the students accomplished with varying degrees of accuracy. In the blue ocean between the two continents, the young artists could use their imagination and artistic freedom to tell the story of an exchange between France and the U.S.

Each of the watercolors is as different as the children, although they all conform to the assignment, which was clearly to show two continents somehow linked. In the example reproduced here, Monique Lavaud painted a brown cargo vessel with three straight lines connecting two red shields, one in the US, the other in France. The lines make the ship appear suspended, transiting the blue ocean like a gondola. Beneath the ship two hands with a U.S. flag on one sleeve and a French flag on the other clasp, linking hands and flags in friendship. Collette Vallet, drew a huge black ship sailing on blue waves beneath a rainbow arch that spans the ocean from New York to Paris. Jeanine Chevalier drew a finely detailed ship flying two French flags leaving Le Havre and a white aircraft hovering above the sea just outside of New York. Monique Mulle drew two white-hulled ships, topped with red and black smokestacks and in clear black ink on the hull, the ships crossing the ocean are named: "Train de l'Amitié" and "Reconnaissance."

Many more works of art, toys, personal and household items that arrived in Lincoln in February 1949, on the Merci Train have been safely stored and exhibited, and many of them can be enjoyed through an on-line exhibit curated by the Nebraska State Museum.

While the Ministry of Agriculture in France had sent trees in every boxcar, not all survived the quarantine period. Some that did are in the park in West Virginia where this boxcar has been beautifully renovated. Photograph courtesy of John Irving.

16. French Trees

The trees that crossed the ocean on the Merci Train were not the first trees to be exchanged in gratitude between France and the United States. The first were tulip trees that George Washington gave to Armand-Charles Tuffin, Marquis de La Rouërie in 1784. The Marquis became somewhat of an

American Revolutionary War hero, but he didn't start out as a hero in France. In fact, Tuffin came to America to redeem himself in the eyes of Louis XVI, whose cousin he had grievously wounded in a duel that followed what was essentially a bar room brawl. To punish the Marquis, the French king banished Tuffin, who had been one of his guards.

In April, of 1777, ten months before the United States and France signed a formal alliance, the Marquis de La Rouërie arrived in America, joined the Continental Army, befriended General George Washington and provided the young Republic with leadership, troops and supplies from abroad. In 1784, Washington expressed his gratitude by giving Tuffin a tree that would grow from a tiny sapling to be one of the tallest of American hardwoods: A Virginia Tulip Tree. On 1 August 1944, as Allied troops under his command fought their way from the beaches of Normandy across France, General John S. "Tiger Jack" Wood roared up the long drive in his military jeep to Saint-Ouen-la-Rouërie, to pay his respects at Washington's Tulip tree.

Five years later, in February 1949, small French Oak Trees were included in the Merci Train, but the scrawny saplings, like all imported plants, were required to undergo a quarantine period and most did not survive. Four little oaks did make the transition in climate and soil and were replanted in West Virginia in a park named Tu-Endie-Wei, which means, "Point Between Two Waters." Decades later, acorns were collected from the mature trees and two of those seedlings found their way to a little town called Welch, where they were planted not far from West Virginia's restored boxcar, waiting in solitary dignity for visitors to wonder where it came from.

BOOK FOUR – EPILOGUE

Friendship & Gratitude

The stories carried in gifts of friendship and gratitude by these two trains are just beginning to surface. There are hundreds. Maybe thousands.

Some of the stories are puzzling. Like the one about David C. White, a generous Kansan from Kingsdown, who donated 7,226 bushels of wheat to the Friendship Train. White was rewarded for his generosity with a tax bill that valued the wheat at $2.65 a bushel, bringing the total donation to just over $19,000.00, on which he owed 50 percent tax. On top of the hefty $8,950 taxes owed, the Internal Revenue Service demanded a $179 late payment penalty.[99] Whether or not

---

[99] *From the Arkansas Traveler, undated. Two clippings that had been cut from newspapers and sent to Pearson were located by Roxanne Godsey among the Drew Pearson papers at the LBJ Library. RG 1928/1929. One note is noted as published in the Arkansas City Traveler; the other is without provenance, and is postmarked July 1948.*

White paid the I.R.S. for his charitable contribution was not published, but one can only hope that common sense prevailed.

Other stories are illustrative of the opposite of generosity: greed. In Europe, it turns out that some of what was given freely in the U.S. got diverted and sold. Pearson's papers include at least one incident that occurred in Italy. Rosalie Rosasco from Waterbury, Connecticut, wrote to Pearson worrying about her aunt in Italy who paid someone 4,000 lire (the equivalent of approximately $80 U.S. today)[100] to receive a package from the Friendship Train and never received anything. Of course, no one had to buy food from the train, so Pearson wrote a long letter back to Ms. Rosasco explaining the distribution process. After a full page about who was getting the food in Italy—(75 percent to children; the rest to the elderly) and who was in charge of parceling it out (four American Relief Agencies cooperating with Italian officials), Pearson ended with, "I am afraid that some officials in Italy are unscrupulous and that your aunt was a victim of them."[101]

It should be noted, too, that France was not the only country to send its thanks. Italy sent four bronze men and horse sculptures that were installed on the Arlington Memorial Bridge and the Theodore Roosevelt Memorial Bridge in Washington D.C. The Netherlands sent a forty-nine-bell carillon whose deep melodic peals can be heard in the capital

---

[100] *The value of Italian lire fluctuated after the end of the war, but using the Bretton Woods System, which was established in November 1947, one US dollar was worth about 575 lire. Adjusted for inflation, one US dollar in 1947 is equal to about $11.34 today, so Rosalie's aunt paid the equivalent of about $80 US for a box of food she never received.*

[101] *From letters in the Drew Pearson archives at the LBJ Library in Austin. RG 1911 and 1917.*

every day as its song drifts from the US Marine Memorial in Arlington Ridge Park across the Potomac. But both of these gifts were government to government. What makes the Merci Train unique is its distinctly person-to-person flavor.

The British bristled at the whole idea of the Merci Train. Sir Edmund Hall-Patch, the British Ambassador to the Organization for European Economic Cooperation, the Paris-based group charged with administering the Marshall Plan, was alarmed to think that the British might be seen as ungrateful. As the *Magellan* carrying the Merci Train docked in New York Harbor in February 1949, he dashed off an urgent letter describing what the French were doing and suggesting that Britain should not be outclassed by the French.

Another official countered, "I must confess that the whole idea is quite repugnant to me and I do not believe it would cut any ice with the Americans...I read a piece about the French gift in *Time* last night and I am bound to say that I did not think they were regarding it as something very effective; they seemed to me rather to regard it, as I do, as rather an indecent joke."[102] He was wrong. Americans celebrated the train and its gifts and all the people who sent them.

OECD Ambassador Hall-Patch later persisted, in trying to convince the British to offer a symbol of gratitude as well. He suggested that Britain should send the Magna Carta on a tour of the U.S. feeling that it would remind Americans of the

---

[102] *Exchange between British diplomats is as reported by A. Mukharji, in Diplomas and Diplomacy, 2016 DOI 10.1057/978-1-137-58653-7_3. Accessed through Google books, December 5, 2018.*

common political traditions shared by the two English-speaking countries, but the legal challenges and political resistance proved insurmountable.

Every boxcar included dozens of dolls from every area of France. Some were made by the famous dollmaker, Juneau, in Paris. Others were carefully handstitched. Photo by Carissa Whiting. Courtesy of the Arizona Capitol Museum, Merci Train Collection.

International relationships are not, perhaps, so very different from personal relationships that are strengthened or severed by gifts wrapped with care or words spoken in haste. Eleanor Roosevelt knew that. She grew up in a privileged family, but her mother was emotionally abusive. Eleanor's father, Elliott, was an alcoholic and drug addict but he deeply loved Eleanor and encouraged her through letters and gifts even after he was banished from the family by his brother. One of the reasons that there were a large number of dolls included on the Merci Train has to do with Eleanor. As one French donor wrote in a letter to Mme. Roosevelt, "Your wish to receive dolls from France as a souvenir in memory of the one your father brought back to you from one of his trips in our country deeply touched the hearts of French children. So, my children worked, sewed, drew, to send you a Dauphiné country woman wearing the costume of a nearby village and in this way thank America as much as they could."[103]

On December 10, 1948, as contributions for the Merci Train continued to pour into collection points across France, Eleanor Roosevelt, who was chair of the United Nations Commission on Human Rights, was in Paris. On that day, fifty-eight nations voted to adopt the Universal Declaration of Human Rights. After the vote, "something happened that never happened in the United Nations before or since. The delegates rose to give a standing ovation to a single delegate, a shy elderly lady with a rather formal demeanor but a very warm smile. Her name, of course, was Eleanor Roosevelt."[104]

Drew Pearson may not have gotten a standing ovation, but in 1949, Senators from both sides of the aisle nominated him for the Nobel Peace Prize. In their nomination, Wayne Morse, Republican from Oregon and James W. Fulbright, Democrat from Arkansas described Pearson as a "journalist and philanthropic agitator." Though he did not win, Pearson was proud of being recognized for what he considered his greatest achievement.

Most Americans have never heard of either the Friendship Train or the Merci Train. That's not surprising. They were small blips of good will following the great turmoil of a World War, and the tempestuous dawn of the nuclear age. They were

---

[103] *This letter is from the Nevada State Merci Train collection, which includes several notes from donors.*
[104] *This account of the day's events at the United Nations is as reported by Richard Gardner in the New York Times, December 10, 1948. Accessed on-line at https://www.nytimes.com/1988/12/10/opinion/eleanor-roosevelt-s-legacy-human-rights.html.*

also not entirely unique. Individuals have always found ways to express their gratitude. During WWI, after Americans sent rations of flour to Belgium that fed ten million civilians for five years in the midst of a war zone, grateful Belgians sometimes returned those empty sacks stitched with ornate and individual messages of thanks.[105]

Still, the food, notes and gifts exchanged between the U.S. and France long ago remain powerful today. They are links across time and distance between nations and families and individuals, who despite differences in language and culture and history and geography, shared—and continue to share— that most powerful ability: to give thanks.

---

[105] *Statistics are from the Herbert Hoover Presidential Library and Museum, https://hoover.archives.gov/exhibits/years-compassion-1914-1923, accessed December 5, 2018.*

Jane Sweetland has degrees in American Studies, counseling, and education and is the author of three non-fiction books. She likes to research, ski, read, hike, bicycle and walk with the dog or friends or family or anyone who will take a moment to notice whatever there is to see. Her family and friends are happily scattered around the world, allowing her to justify traveling anywhere any time. She lives at Lake Tahoe, Nevada